Table of Contents

Tables

Acronyms

ANA	Afghanistan National Army
ANP	Afghanistan National Police
ANSF	Afghanistan National Security Forces
AO	Area of Operation
ASP	Afghanistan Solidarity Program
BATT	British Army Training Team
CAS	Close Air Support
CAT	Civil Action Team
CENTCOM	Central Command
CERP	Commanders Emergency Response Program
COE	Contemporary Operating Environment
COIN	Counterinsurgency
COP	Combat Outpost
DEV	Development
DLF	Dhofar Liberation Front
DOD	Department of Defense
DSO	Distinguished Service Order
DWEC	District War Executive Committee
FOB	Forward Operating Base
FWC	Federal War Council
GOV	Governance
GWOT	Global War On Terrorism
IO	Information Operations
ISAF	International Security and Assistance Force
MC	Military Cross
MCP	Malayan Communist Party
MID	Mentioned in Dispatches
MM	Military Medal
MPAJA	Malayan People's Anti-Japanese Army
MRLA	Malayan Races Liberation Army
OEF	Operation Enduring Freedom
OIF	Operation Iraqi Freedom
PDRY	People's Democratic Republic Yemen

PFLOAG	Popular Front Liberation Occupied Arab Gulf
PFLO	Popular Front Liberation Oman
PSYOPS	Psychological Operations
ROE	Rules of Engagement
SAF	Sultan's Armed Forces
SAS	Special Air Service
SEC	Security
SEP	Surrendered Enemy Personnel
SWEC	State War Executive Committee
TTP	Tactics, Techniques, and Procedures
USAID	United States Agency International Development

Chapter 1

Introduction

All successful counterinsurgents have been willing and able to kill the enemy, often with great ruthlessness but all have clearly distinguished that enemy from the population in which it hides, have applied violence as precisely and carefully as possible, have acted scrupulously within the law, and have emphasized measures to protect and win over the population.

— David Kilcullen,
Counterinsurgency

Over the past 10 years of war in Afghanistan, a philosophical debate has emerged as to which counterinsurgency approach most readily produces favorable outcomes: population-centric or enemy-centric. Population-centric counterinsurgency (COIN) touts partnering with and protecting the population from the enemy, whereas enemy-centric COIN emphasizes the importance of focusing all effort on killing and capturing the enemy.[1]

A third school of thought deems neither approach appropriate when executed in isolation, but advocates a balanced strategy customized for each area of operation's dynamics. The debate over adopting a population-centric versus an enemy-centric strategy is multidimensional, and not remotely black and white. It is grey. Each approach contains critical elements necessary to success. As David Kilcullen's quotation indicates, successful counterinsurgents both aggressively pursue the enemy and protect the population, integrating both strategies.

This thesis examines the views of both the traditional and counterinsurgency war theorists and investigates three complex counterinsurgency campaigns in order to get to the heart of this debate and uncover the truths that will carry us forward in the years ahead. The war experience of the theorists coupled with the detailed analysis of counterinsurgency strategy in the Malaya, Oman, and Afghanistan campaigns provides evidence that integrating the enemy-centric and population-centric strategies into a balanced, hybrid approach affords counterinsurgents a real opportunity to succeed in the contemporary operating environment (COE).

Research Goal

The debate between an enemy-centric and population-centric counterinsurgency approach in the contemporary operating environment is a polarizing and ineffective one.[2] The COE in Afghanistan is complex. Solutions necessarily get tailored to local areas, requiring vastly different approaches at the tactical level to achieve success. A strategy which yields a resounding victory in one enclave of Afghanistan may precipitate devastating defeat twenty miles over the next rise because, in this conflict, political landscape and context reign supreme. These approaches must constantly morph to outpace the enemy and account for the shifting attitudes within the population.

Commanders must have the clearance to tactically pivot to address counterinsurgent activities in each area of operation (AO) without fear of their actions being cherry picked to support the counterinsurgency theory of the day back home. Although there is constant thirst for a common solution to defeat the insurgency, there is no fail-safe solution to quench it.[3] Whether a commander focuses on the enemy, the population, or both is largely decided by local conditions at the time. Each area represents diverse challenges with respect to the local people, the enemy, governance, culture, and socio-economic conditions that require commanders to formulate specialized approaches to best address the situation in their areas. We must drop the "centric" banners from our lexicon and embrace a balanced campaign methodology. Integrate elements of national power, deliver assets from across the lines of effort (security, economy, development, governance, psychological) in the measured doses conducive to defeating the enemy while supporting the local population and each commander, at his respective echelon, and the counterinsurgency effort overall just might prevail. Finally, interventionist powers such as the US in Afghanistan must ensure its counterinsurgency strategy is aligned and nested with the host nation's to facilitate its political end state.

Importance

This study's findings illuminate a number of important issues. First, close examination of the war theorists' work suggests the focus on the population and the enemy have never been mutually exclusive in war. The counterinsurgency campaigns in both Malaya and Dhofar, Oman demonstrate that if a strategy leans too heavily toward killing and capturing the enemy or favors the population to the exclusion of enemy pursuit, progress is hobbled.[4] The Malaya and Oman campaigns were specifically selected for this study because they are British campaigns conducted on vastly different scales. Malaya was highly organized and resourced while Oman was more decentralized with scarce resources. The juxtaposition of these conflicts offers a unique view of British application of national power. More importantly, Malaya was selected because U.S military circles often refer to it as an example of a population-centric, "Hearts and Minds," campaign.[5] Once analyzed in greater depth the evidence is much greyer, suggesting success against the insurgency emerged only once a balanced strategy that leveraged intelligence-driven offensive operations against the enemy while simultaneously integrating other resources across the lines of effort in the appropriate weighted way conducive to the local area and time was attained. Oman was selected because, within the US, it is not a well known COIN campaign. It was small scale but offered lessons similar to Malaya's, particularly in terms of the formulating strategy, even though these counterinsurgencies took place within vastly different contexts and political landscapes. A balanced strategy integrating all resources across the lines of effort, both in support of the population and against the insurgency, appears to have been effective in these historical case studies.

In Afghanistan, it took nearly nine years of war to attain some semblance of a balanced approach after initially adopting an enemy-centric approach, changing course to a population-centric strategy, and finally rebalancing tactical efforts to include a hybrid approach. While the war is not over and it does not seem that victory is over the horizon, the current balanced approach offers the most flexibility for success there. The crucial point in this study is that there is no panacea for success in countering an insurgency.

The strategies that facilitated the quickest path to defeating the respective insurgencies or forced a political solution were balanced; however, each case study was different due to the context of the forces arrayed on both sides of the campaign. The counterinsurgents mobilized elements of national power and both utilized resources against the insurgency and in support of the population, based on local conditions. When the approach is combined, balanced, and synchronized to address sociological dynamics on the ground, a counterinsurgency strategy is created that offers the most promising way ahead. A commander cannot say what his winning strategy will look like when he first arrives to his post and he should not promote his unique approach as a fix-all upon his successful mission completion. These issues are complicated and their resolution depends heavily upon intuitive and responsive strategy development. The need for adaptive officers capable of applying unique balanced approaches weighted appropriately to fit their respective AOs is critical to success. We are only as effective as our commanders' assessments of their AOs. The U.S military, policy makers and strategists should rethink their narratives and possibly abandon the "centric" narrative because it complicates forging ahead with a balanced strategy that gives commanders at every level the necessary autonomy to accomplish their missions and expedite a political solution.

Thesis Overview:

This thesis consists of six major sections. Chapter 1 contains the research goal, importance and thesis overview. Chapter 2 reviews both traditional and counterinsurgency war theorists. Chapter 3, 4, and 5 consist of the case studies of Malaya, Oman, and the contemporary operating environment (COE) in Afghanistan, respectively. Chapter 6 synthesizes and analyzes the case studies in order to recommend a way ahead and highlight the best counterinsurgency approach for use in the COE. Finally, the bibliography section contains the research methodology and an alphabetical listing of sources by last name in each respective periodical type.

Notes

1.   There is no published definition for either population-centric or enemy-centric counterinsurgency in US doctrine. In the absence of these definitions, the following definition is offered: Population-centric COIN focuses on partnering with and protecting the population from the enemy. While enemy destruction is still important, it is secondary to population protection. Enemy-centric COIN focuses effort on the killing and capturing of the enemy while population protection is of secondary importance.

2.   To better understand the debate between population and enemy-centric COIN, read the ISAF tactical directives describing the implementation of population-centric COIN including, "Tactical Directive," Kabul, AF: International Security and Assistance Force, July 6, 2009 and the "ISAF Commander's Counterinsurgency Guidance," *International Security Assistance Force,* August 26, 2009. Also read Binard Finel's "A substitute for Victory," in *Foreign Affairs,* April 8, 2010; that supports population-centric COIN as the strategy in Afghanistan. To understand both arguments against population-centric COIN and for an enemy-centric approach, read Colonel Gian Gentile's "A Strategy of Tactics: Population-centric COIN and the Army," in *Parameters,* Autumn 2009 and Colonel Craig Collier's "Now That We're Leaving Iraq, What Did We Learn," *Military Review,* September-October 2010.

3.   The case studies will clearly prove that there is no silver-bullet approach that produces immediate success in counterinsurgency.

4.   Review chapter 3 and 4, Malaya and Oman respectively, for a more nuanced understanding of how the strategies evolved from an approach heavily focused on killing the enemy to a more balanced approach integrating all resources available, effectively isolating and destroying the insurgency while partnering with and protecting the civilian population.

5.   Read Colonel Gian Gentile's "A Strategy of Tactics: Population-centric COIN and the Army," in *Parameters,* Autumn 2009, 6 or look at the US Army's FM 3-24, Counterinsurgency Manual, which discusses "true" definition of hearts and minds on page A-5.

Chapter 2
Insurgency And Counterinsurgency, and the Classification of 'Centric' Operations

Revolutionaries will have to start from nothing. Starting from nothing initially requires organization. Secretly, the revolutionaries have to organize, first, cells and then, extensive networks of conspiracy. Around the cells they must build political propaganda groups to win popular support and teams of terrorists to intimidate where propaganda fails. They will organize fronts, parties, and pressure groups to mobilize the popular support. Agents will be infiltrated into the administration, armed forces, police, labour unions and other power centres. Intelligence networks will be established. . . . All cracks in the social and administrative structures will be magnified and exploited.

— John McCuen,
The Art of Counter-Revolutionary War

This chapter analyzes the theory of warfare, insurgency, and counterinsurgency as described by both the classical and contemporary theorists. The definition of both insurgency and counterinsurgency will establish a common understanding prior to the review and analysis of the theorists' methodologies. The theorists assert that in every war, regardless of whether the conflict is a conventional war or a counterinsurgency, all elements of national strategy (political, economic, social, governmental, and psychological) are utilized. The theorists' volumes of research prove there is no 'centric' side of war; thus the debate between the population-centric and the enemy-centric camps is neither valid nor black and white. War is war. It requires the application of different elements of national power to suit the local situation. The current debate will be presented on counterinsurgency strategy executed in Afghanistan between the population and enemy centric camps through the lens of the theorists.

Insurgency and Counterinsurgency: The Definitions

Insurgency and subversion are not a new phenomenon. The last decade of conflict has forced the United States and other countries to re-examine the capability of modern groups, how to deal with insurgents, and to re-evaluate its own capacity to counter these movements. A thorough examination of the historical counterinsurgency theorists' assertions, below, has led me to Sir General Frank Kitson's widely agreed upon definition of insurgency and subversion.[1]

Defining both insurgency and subversion separately provides the most comprehensive definition available.

Subversion, then, will be held to mean all measures short of the use of armed force taken by one section of the people of a country to overthrow those governing the country at the time, or to force them to do things which they do not want to do. It can involve the use of political and economic pressure, strikes, protest marches, propaganda, and can also include the use of small-scale violence for the purpose of coercing recalcitrant members of the population into giving support. Insurgency will be held to cover the use of armed force by a section of the people against the government for the purposes mentioned above.[2]

Where an insurgency brews there is often a counterinsurgency effort, waged by the ruling government party, group in charge, an interventionist power, or a combination of players. Although many conflicts between insurgents and counterinsurgents begin because of deep asymmetries between the two, there is often great commonality in the strategies each must pursue to win or reach a settlement.[3] The insurgents and counterinsurgents find themselves competing for many of the same goals such as the right to govern, the support of the population, and control of resources and economic opportunities. Some insurgencies are regionally based and simply desire the central government or ruling power to stay out of their areas and not exert state control over their people.[4] Counterinsurgency is best defined by David Kilcullen[5] as "an umbrella term that describes the complete range of measures that governments take to defeat insurgencies. These measures may be political, administrative, military, economic, psychological, or informational, and are almost always used in combination."[6]

Foundations of Warfare Theory

The foundation of insurgency and counterinsurgency theory share the same roots that all types of warfare share. Sun-Tzu, a Chinese Military General who wrote *The Art of War* twenty five centuries ago, described the principles of warfare then as eloquently as anyone could today. Sun-Tzu understood the political process was the most important aspect of warfare and that armed conflict only came after all other avenues had been explored and exhausted. National political cohesion could only be achieved "under a government which was devoted to the people's welfare and did not oppress them….war [was inextricably linked] to the immediate political process."[7] He believed in the power of negotiation and reaching consensus to reach the political and military objective prior to war. He stated "[if] the moral strength and intellectual faculty of man were decisive in war, and that if these were properly applied war could be waged with certain success."[8] After a concerted effort to avoid armed conflict using all other means available, be it political, economic, psychological, or deceptive, armed aggression became necessary to achieve the will of the state or ruler. "Armed force . . . was applied so that victory was gained: (1) in the shortest time possible; (2) at the least possible cost in lives and effort; (3) with infliction on the enemy of the fewest possible casualties."[9]

Sun-Tzu highlights popular support as an essential foundation for a nation's success in war. Although he discusses popular support in context as related to the ruling party or nation, this truth is obviously essential to both the insurgent or counterinsurgent camps. He understood the importance of intelligence as he launched agents to infiltrate his foes; speed and surprise exploited his enemies' vulnerability. Sun-Tzu knew the commanders' capacity to adapt quickly to changing situations and operating environments was crucial. He determined whether to wage war by carefully considering foes' relative strengths and capabilities and he scrutinized the following five areas: "human (morale and generalship), physical (terrain and weather), and doctrinal."[10] Unless his Army was clearly superior in all five arenas, Sun-Tzu avoided war.

Antoine-Henri Jomini, a French General who served in both the French and Russian militaries from 1798 until his retirement in 1829, was a celebrated military strategist who analyzed the Napoleonic way of war which many credit as establishing the framework for western war structure. Unlike Sun-Tzu and Clausewitz, who closely analyzed the theory of war, Jomini focused on the science of war, the synchronization of the battlefield, and the tactical and operational mechanical maneuvers and coordination of military forces against the enemy. This is reinforced as Jomini discussed the nature of the art of war. "The art of war, independently of its political and moral relations, consists of five principal parts, viz.: Strategy, Grand Tactics, Logistics, Tactics of the different arms, and the Art of the Engineer."[11]

Many of the basic tactical and operational maneuver lessons and mechanisms Jomini branded, especially in the "first half of the 19th Century,"[12] such as operating from interior lines, protecting lines of communication, combined arms synchronization, offensive order of battle and defensive engagement area development, heavily influence Western and US doctrine today. Jomini understood the critical interplay of political strategy and warfare. He states there is an "intimate connection between statesmanship and war in its preliminaries, [and] in most campaigns some military enterprises are undertaken to carry out a political end, sometimes quite important, but often very irrational. They frequently lead to the commission of great errors in strategy."[13] If political objectives and military strategy are not harmonious, the campaign effort is doomed from the start.

We may place the passions of the nation to be fought, their military system, their immediate means and their reserves, their financial resources, the attachment they bear to their government or their institutions, the character of the executive, the characters and military abilities of the commanders of their armies, the influence of cabinet councils or councils of war at the capital upon their operations, the system of war in favor with their staff, the established force of the state and its armament, the military geography and statistics of the state which is to be invaded, and, finally, the resources and obstacles of every kind likely to be met with, all of which are included neither in diplomacy nor in strategy.[14]

Although Jomini's description points to another state in his analysis of determining whether or not to go to war, the principles regarding political objectives and military calculations are the same today whether we are planning a conventional war or a counterinsurgency effort.[15]

Jomini does discuss insurgency in his book *The Art of War;* however, he describes it through the lens of his time as an internal uprising of the population because of "political or religious sectarianism."[16] He states, "Intestine wars, when not connected with a foreign quarrel, are generally the result of a conflict of opinions. . . . Governments may in good faith intervene to prevent the spreading of a political disease whose principles threaten social order."[17] The important point here is that nowhere in Jomini's book *Art of War* does he attempt to classify internal conflict or intervention on behalf of another state as anything but war. All flavors and levels of war require a political strategy and support and the means to accomplish the political and military objectives.

Carl Von Clausewitz, a Prussian General who served in both the Prussian and Russian military from 1792 until his death in 1831, is credited with writing *On War,* originally published in 1874, which stands as the Western world's foremost illustration of the philosophy of war. Clausewitz famously states "war is simply a continuation of political intercourse, with the addition of other means."[18] His description and application of the principles and theories of war have served as a guidepost for some Western militaries since *On War* was published and have been aptly applied in

10

all types of warfare whether total or against a "general uprising."[19]. As Sun-Tzu believed, Clausewitz understood the importance of mass, speed, surprise, cunning, and the flexibility and mental acuity of leaders in war. He warns against blind compliance with doctrine, noting that each war, each area of operation, is different with unique circumstances to consider. He accurately asserts that the study of theory, rather than a reliance on doctrine, is critically important to the development and education of a leader and can be better applied to the changing nature of warfare in the future.

We must remind ourselves that it is simply not possible to construct a model for the art of war that can serve as a scaffolding on which the commander can rely for support at any time. Whenever he has to fall back on his innate talent, he will find himself outside the model and in conflict with it; no matter how versatile the code, the situation will always lead to the consequences we have already alluded to: talent and genius operate outside the rules, and theory conflicts with practice.[20]

Clausewitz, in the 19th Century, understood the emerging phenomenon of modern insurgency in Europe. He believed "a general insurrection [was] simply another means of war."[21] He understood that if an insurgency was to be successful, it needed time, space, sanctuary, and dispersion to cultivate popular support, to arm and train its members, and to increase in strength. He realized that an insurgency was best put down at its inception and, if overlooked, a popular uprising could become a real threat to the state.

No matter how brave a people is, how warlike its traditions, how great its hatred for the enemy, how favorable the ground on which it fights: the fact remains that a national uprising cannot maintain itself where the atmosphere is too full of danger . . . if its fuel is to be fanned into a major conflagration, it must be at some distance, where there is enough air, and the uprising cannot be smothered by a single smoke.[22]

Clausewitz describes the most effective route to success for an insurgency facing a more powerful enemy is to attack supply lines in the rear while disallowing itself to be decisively engaged, only concentrating force on vulnerable formations, remaining both transitory and illusory all the while. "The element of resistance will exist everywhere and nowhere."[23] He describes the conditions that must exist to enable an insurgency's success.

Table 1. Conditions under which a general uprising can be effective
1. The war must be fought in the interior of the country.
2. It must not be decided by a single stroke.
3. The theater of operations must be fairly large.
4. The national character must be suited to that type of war.
5. The country must be rough and inaccessible, because of mountains, of forests, marshes, or the local methods of cultivation.

Source: Carl Von Clausewitz, *On War* (Princeton, NJ: Princeton University Press, 1976), 480.

Just as Clausewitz prescribed enduring principles of war that hold true today, he also clearly established that war is war; a popular uprising or insurgency is no different. Each conflict is unique, forcing a state to apply different means in each to regain control and defeat the threat. One must "act on the principle of using no greater force, and setting himself no greater military aim, than would be sufficient for the achievement of his political purpose."[24] Whether the state finds itself engaged in total or limited war against another state, or against a general uprising of the population, it must apply means to counter the threat to win the conflict or force a settlement. Every war in history has proven that.

Sun-Tzu, Jomini, and Clausewitz each approach the concept of warfare differently. Sun-Tzu and Clausewitz focus on the theory of war while Jomini describes the more rigid doctrine and science of war. Even though these theorists' perspectives were shaped through varied experiences, cultures, and in the case of Sun-Tzu, vastly disparate timeframes, each acknowledges that the conduct of war is connected to political objectives. They all discuss the potential for insurrection, popular uprising, or insurgency to develop. More importantly, they do not classify these conditions as anything other than war. Sun-Tzu states "As water has no constant form, there are in war no constant conditions."[25] He understood the support of the population was necessary in any conflict and a general uprising of the people could be disastrous. He grasped that each conflict was different, possessing its own unique context that describes war. Jomini also describes war and politics as inseparable and links "Diplomacy in its relation to War. . . . It enters into all the combinations which may lead to a war, and has a connection with the various operations to be undertaken."[26] He points to the threat of internal uprising, or intestine wars, and simply warns it is another type of war. Finally, Clausewitz discusses the potential for insurgency, directly addressing the debate on whether or not to commit the state's forces to quell an insurgency. "The resources expended in an insurrection might be put to better use in other kinds of warfare."[27] To these classical theorists, war, no matter how big or small, is simply war.

Insurgency and Counterinsurgency Theorists

The Insurgency Camp

Insurgencies, popular uprisings, and revolutions have increased dramatically since the end of the Second World War. There are a number of mutually supporting theories that explain why. The first theory suggests the "crumbling of European empires under colonial and even domestic assault, and the rapid appearance amidst the imperial ruins of new successor states,"[28] have fueled the conditions for insurgency and revolution. Internal and external conflict naturally occur as a result of independent states emerging from colonial rule and struggling to establish their own identities and governments. This, coupled with globalization and rapid advancements in technology including nuclear weapons, has essentially shrunk the world. Today traditional powers going to war with one another must weigh the benefit against the inherently dear costs of such action. "Globalisation changed the nature of the conflict area, strengthening some actors, weakening others and altering the conditions of the conflict between government forces and insurgents to favour the latter."[29] There is not one theory that is wholly responsible for the rise in subversion and insurgency throughout the world as each conflict area has its own unique history.

It is hard to think of a greater revolutionary leader than Mao Tse-Tung. Mao, a military leader and member of China's communist party, used the principles of Sun-Tzu to create the foundation for his concept of guerrilla warfare, described in his book *On Guerrilla Warfare*, mobilizing the local Chinese population to achieve victory over the Chinese Nationalist Party in 1949. Mao's real genius was displayed "in Indochina, where the Vietnamese waged a revolutionary struggle against the French from 1941 to 1954."[30] It is from this conflict, and the refinements later made by Giap, who is discussed in detail in the coming pages, from which the concept of "Maoism" is best understood.[31] Mao appreciated the importance of mobilizing the local population and garnering their political support around a rallying political objective. His concept of guerrilla warfare, which we would now refer to as insurgency, was not a purely military affair. His strategy involved a wide range of social, psychological, political, and military components working in unity with each other. Mao understood that once he had the popular and political support of the people, he could then begin to organize them into active guerrilla units to carry out the military phase of his strategy.

Table 2. How Guerrilla Units Are Originally Formed
The unit may originate in any one of the following ways:
a) From the masses of the people.
b) From regular army units temporarily detailed for the purpose.
c) From regular army units permanently detailed.
d) From the combination of the regular army unit and a unit recruited from the local people.
e) From the local militia.
f) From deserters from the ranks of the enemy.
g) From former bandits and bandit groups.

Source: Mao Tse-Tung, *On Guerrilla Warfare* (New York: Praeger Publishers, 1961), 71-72.

Mao's military strategy is most recognized for his unique three-phased approach. It is important to understand that Mao's three phases did not progress sequentially in time and space. The progression, or regression, of the phases were a direct reflection of enemy strength, activity, and strategy and would be adjusted to best counter it.

The first phase ought to consist of isolated hit-and-run attacks against enemy forces, with the aim of weakening and demoralizing them. The second phase would witness the consolidation of guerrilla power in some remote, outlying and difficult area to access; from there they would continue their work of propaganda, harassment and sabotage . . . the third phase of their campaign, would resort to open warfare.[32]

Mao considered the support of the local population throughout each of the phases. He directed his fighters to work under a strict and honorable code when dealing with civilians. They had to be perceived by the locals as the better future alternative to the existing government structure. Mao also released strict guidelines on the treatment of enemy personnel. He believed they had to be treated with dignity and respect; they were a potential asset to use against the enemy still in the field.[33]

Mao's three-phased military strategy was one of the most effective guerrilla strategies ever implemented. As important as it was, the military strategy could not have been successful without first mobilizing the population and garnering local political support. "The political goal must be clearly and precisely indicated to inhabitants of guerrilla zones and their national consciousness awakened."[34] Mao clearly surmised that the strategy was not purely military. It was critical to maintain the people's support, using all means available to him, whether enacting local government, social, economic, political or military means.[35]

General Vo Nguyen Giap, the Vietnamese People's Army leader, credited with assisting in the defeat of the Japanese in 1945 the French in Vietnam in 1954, was heavily influenced by Sun Tzu and Mao in his approach to guerrilla warfare.[36] After expelling the Japanese from China in 1945, General Giap, together with Ho Chi Mihn, turned his attention to the defeat of the French.[37] Giap led a protracted insurgent campaign that culminated with the massive defeat of French forces at Dien Bien Phu in May of 1954. Giap stated " the Dien Bien victory is the most prestigious which our Army has ever achieved . . . we have expanded our zone of resistance and further contributed to the success of land reform . . . In the name of the Army I warmly thank all the porters and the whole population."[38]

General Giap's view, comparable to Mao, recognized the importance of the local population's political and social support. He understood the victory against the French was not the result of a purely military strategy. He had orchestrated total war that required all of the elements at his disposal to work in conjunction for victory. He leveraged local governance and social reform, psychological operations, and convinced the local population they were better off without French interference to achieve active popular support. As the French gave up their aspirations in Indochina, fueled by the loss at Dien Bien Phu, Giap's reputation among the people grew exponentially.[39]

When the US combat formations entered Vietnam in 1965, Giap already had over a decade of experience leading guerrilla movements. Armed with his vast experience, he devised a strategy based on Mao's three-phased approach to defeat the US Phase one of the strategy included "a general offensive against South Vietnamese cities."[40] The idea was that the South Vietnamese military would be forced to protect the cities, leaving the rural areas open for the Viet Cong to easily influence. In the second phase, if "the general offensive failed, Viet Cong troops would retreat, surrounding the cities and villages to create a chaotic situation, to exhaust the economy."[41] Simultaneously, Viet Cong forces would concentrate their efforts on specific areas, forcing the US to reinforce those areas leaving other areas more vulnerable to attack. In the final phase, the North Vietnamese would initiate a large scale attack that would catch the US off balance. Giap believed the first two phases of the campaign would cause such turmoil that a successful large scale attack, timed appropriately, would force political settlement. The important aspect of the strategy was that the phases were not sequential and were wedded to the action of the enemy.[42]

General Giap launched the Tet Offensive in January 1968. The offensive had a psychological effect in the United States although his Army had an unsustainable casualty rate against the Americans. The scale of the attack was "spectacular enough to dominate television attention long enough to make an impact of strength on the American public. . . . By overrunning the towns. . . . Giap shattered what confidence many people had left in American power to win a military victory in Vietnam."[43] The political situation on both sides was complicated after the Tet offensive. Giap would face harsh criticism for the large casualty toll inflicted on his forces as a result of Tet and subsequently lose political power in Hanoi.

Although the The Tet offensive ultimately proved to be a political victory for the Communists, militarily it was a disaster. Heavy losses led the Communists to withdraw some of their major units to remote base camps and cross-border sanctuaries far from South Vietnam's population centers. . . .Ironically, the Communist offensive had achieved what MACV had only imperfectly accomplished after three years of effort-it had driven the main force units back and weakened the remaining guerrillas to the extent that pacification could finally move forward.[44]

It would take years for the psychological effect that the offensive had on the American psyche to be realized; however, Giap's objective to decrease US public opinion would prove to have been successful over time.[45] The US had won the battle but the violent images of Tet back in the US strengthened the veracity of the anti-war debate and resulted in a wholesale change of leadership in the US Army. Giap's three-phased strategy framework would be carried on by subsequent commanders. Although the war would rage on for seven more years, the framework, coupled with the support of the population and an effective propaganda campaign, would ultimately drive the US to leave in 1975.

Mao Tse-Tung and Vo Nguyen Giap executed more than just military strategies. They both showed great expertise by utilizing all elements at their disposal to achieve their political and military objectives. They garnered support from the local populations in the rural areas, inserted local governance, and employed propaganda to strengthen their positions. They understood the necessity to maintain popular support, only using coercive tactics against the locals when absolutely necessary. They realized the limits of their guerrilla forces and avoided large-scale conflict with the enemy. Their military forces chose when and where they fought. They maintained the initiative in the field against a larger and more powerful foe. Most importantly, they did not lose sight of their political objectives and utilized all elements of their national power to achieve victory.

The British Counterinsurgency Camp

The British have a wealth of experience fighting protracted counterinsurgency campaigns, especially since the end of World War II. In an analysis of British counterinsurgency campaigns between 1945 and 2011, the British have been actively involved in counterinsurgency efforts each of those years, many times executing multiple campaigns simultaneously. These campaigns include Greece, Palestine, Aden, Malaya, Kenya, Cyprus, Oman, Malaya, Northern Ireland, Iraq, and Afghanistan.[46] The British experience has highlighted the degree of government involvement necessary for integration with the military in counterinsurgency campaigns. It provided numerous case-studies of both successful and non-successful campaigns that contribute important lessons for governments that face insurgencies in the future. Close examination of the British experience can prevent future counterinsurgency programs from repeating the same mistakes and, at the same time, provide instructive lessons. "There is no easy or quick answer as to how to defeat insurgents, but much can be learned from a study of the many campaigns that have occurred in the past."[47] To wit, a number of British counterinsurgency theorists have emerged throughout these conflicts contributing a wealth of applicable theory.

It is difficult to find a theorist with as much experience as Sir General Frank Kitson. Kitson, a professional Army soldier and counterinsurgent theorist who served in the British Army for 40 years serving "in four separate operational theaters: Kenya, Malaya, Oman, and Cyprus,"[48] has greatly influenced western counterinsurgency theory and practice. Among his numerous publications, he contributed two books dedicated to counterinsurgency, *Low Intensity Operations and Bunch of Five.* Kitson's book, *Bunch of Five,* adds important counterinsurgency tactics, techniques, and procedures (TTPs), describing in detail the four counterinsurgency campaigns he navigated that illuminate the context necessary to understand the lessons he learned, which he had explained in his earlier book, *Low Intensity Operations.*

Kitson has the innate ability to analyze theory and transform it into a palatable framework practitioners can evaluate for future application.

Kitson believes one must address four critical areas when planning to counter an insurgency. He equates these four areas with the four sides of a picture frame, describing how each side must work in conjunction with the others to stay bound together. "The first requirement for a workable campaign is good coordinating machinery."[49] At all levels of command a functioning, cohesive team understands it takes all of the government's resources, political, economic, developmental, or psychological, working in unison to achieve the desired end state. He describes insurgency as another form of warfare. "The main characteristic which distinguishes campaigns of insurgency from other forms of war is that they are primarily concerned with the struggle for men's minds."[50] In each campaign Kitson fought, the local situation and context dictated how the lethal and non-lethal resources at his disposal were applied.

The second part of the framework is "establishing the sort of political atmosphere within which the government measures can be introduced with the maximum likelihood of success."[51] The one advantage the government has over the insurgency is its resources. In most cases the insurgency simply cannot compete with the government's ability to spend. This advantage makes it critically important for the government to analyze the second and third order effects of each measure it introduces and creates an environment in which each measure has the highest potential for success. These measures include everything from security initiatives, economy, development, or psychological operations. Kitson clearly recognized the difficulty in understanding local area contexts and how each mix of government measures would work differently in each area. For this to be successful, Kitson called upon reform in training the Officer Corps. He called for "generally increasing the time allocated to teaching counter-subversion and counter-insurgency in schools and colleges throughout the army."[52]

The third piece of the frame was intelligence. "It is absolutely necessary to understand the fact that the main responsibility for developing background information rests with operational commanders and not with the intelligence organization."[53] Kitson devotes a significant proportion of his writings to how units at all levels must reform their intelligence organizations to suit local conditions and provide the appropriate intelligence support at the most important and relevant levels. Traditionally, intelligence organizations are constructed to provide the weight of the intelligence from the top down. Kitson agrees that information and intelligence at the top is important but he also recognizes the critical need for intelligence at the lower levels to support every echelon of command.

18

In a number counterinsurgency and counter-subversion environments, intelligence at the local level is critical to the success of the campaign. "The intelligence organization must enlarge itself rapidly, must decentralize in order to give security force commanders at every level access to it, and must change its methods of working so as to produce the different sort of information that operational forces need."[54]

The last aspect of Kitson's framework involves the law, which is critical to enabling all of the government efforts to function as intended. Western countries follow strict laws and guidelines, such as the Geneva Convention, that govern how they will conduct themselves and operate in a campaign. Breaking the law is out of the question; however, changing the law to support the counterinsurgency effort and minimize insurgent advantage is encouraged. "It is therefore perfectly normal for governments not only to introduce Emergency Regulations as an insurgency progresses, but also to counter advantages which the insurgents may derive from."[55] Operate inside the confines of the law but change it to give the strategy you are implementing the best chance of success.

Kitson's understanding of the unique requirements at each level of command within a counterinsurgency environment makes his work timeless. Few theorists can provide both the conceptual lessons and the pragmatic, tactical and operational application, or ways, for practitioners to approach campaigns. Kitson stresses that the business of counterinsurgency is not easy and requires considerable study by those involved. Commanders must understand that different sets of skills are required for both them and their subordinates in a counterinsurgency environment. Even so, most commanders train their units for the conventional war and convince themselves it is enough.

Traditionally a soldier is trained and conditioned to be strong, courageous, direct, and aggressive, but when men endowed with these qualities become involved in fighting subversion they often find that their good points are exploited by the enemy...Gradually the more intelligent officers find themselves developing a new set of characteristics such as deviousness, patience, and a determination to outwit their opponents by all means compatible with the achievement of the aim.[56]

Kitson understood that war primarily involving subversion and insurgency was a different kind of war, but it was war. It required the counterinsurgents to conceptualize and approach it differently.

Sir Robert Thompson served both as a district administrator in the Malaya Emergency in the 1950's and as an advisor to the US military and South Vietnamese government in the early 1960's. Thompson's primary contribution to counterinsurgency theory is his book, *Defeating Communist Insurgency*, which he published in 1966 after completing his assignment in Vietnam. Thompson's views on insurgency are heavily influenced by his experiences witnessing communist backed insurgencies in Malaya and Vietnam. He cites the root causes of the insurgencies in Malaya and Vietnam as a result of "anti-colonialism"[57] in Malaya and "anti-imperialism"[58] in Vietnam. He spends a considerable amount of time explaining how insurgencies take root among populations and how they spread. Similar to Kitson, he warns that insurgent intimidation, directed violence, and propaganda heavily influence the actions of the masses and that the government or intervening authority must do all within its power to separate the people and the insurgency before it generates a large popular support base and gains strength.

Thompson offers five principles for governments that must organize to face insurgencies. The first is that the "government must have a clear political aim; to establish and maintain a free, independent and united country which is politically and economically stable and viable."[59] The government's political objective and the associated unity of effort required to achieve it are critically important for success. Equally important is the government's willingness to address the grievances of the insurgency and be open to political compromise. As we will see in our case studies, political compromise is a critical component in successful counterinsurgency campaigns such as Malaya and Dhofar, Oman, discussed at length in the coming chapters. Thompson names three factors that influence the citizens of a nation, "nationalism and national policies, religion and customs, material well-being and progress."[60] The population wants to be associated with the side they believe will be prosperous, victorious, and offer the best social and economic alternative for the future.

The second principle is that the "government must function in accordance with the law."[61] As with Kitson, Thompson places great emphasis on the criticality of the government operating within the confines of the law. He re-emphasizes the point that the law should not inhibit operations but, rather, facilitate them. If the laws in place impede the government's ability to succeed, those laws must be changed. In the British tradition, this was dealt with by enacting emergency laws and regulations for the duration of the conflict. New laws in the form of emergency regulations could range from draconian to empowering. The most important lesson Thompson learned when applying emergency regulations was "each new law must be effective and fairly applied."[62]

The third principle states "The government must have an overall plan. This plan must cover not just the security measures and military operations. It must include all political, social, economic, administrative, police and other measures which have a bearing on the insurgency."[63] The integration of the civilian authorities executing many of the political, social, and administrative activities with the military executing security and aspects of all the other measures is, at the least, difficult. If unity of effort is not achieved, a cohesive plan that avoids "duplication of effort" between civilian and military authorities is not possible.[64]

The fourth principle dictates "the government must give priority to defeating the political subversion, not the guerillas."[65] It is obviously important to destroy guerilla forces whenever making contact with them. The hard part is actually finding them as the guerillas avoid pitched battles with better armed government forces. What the government can do, and do very successfully, is to regain the lost influence they had within the population and win back the villages, towns, and cities by placing great weight on the establishment of responsive local and regional governance. A responsive government, backed by a hefty purse, can bring tangible services to areas in a way insurgents simply cannot. This is significant. As the government directs its efforts to bolster local governance and services, the insurgency will begin to lose its hold on the local population. Lose the local political support of the population and the insurgents' power wanes.[66]

The fifth principle states "In the guerilla phase of an insurgency, a government must secure its base areas first."[67] The military forces must guard against getting spread too thin. A viable security force must be established to repel insurgent attacks against each installation the government possesses. This can be accomplished in a number of ways, whether through the training of local indigenous forces to serve as a home guard, host nation security forces, or police. Thompson goes on to describe that securing these base areas is important enough to execute even if it means allowing the insurgency to retain freedom of maneuver in the remote areas. If the government forces are not large or powerful enough to control the entire area, it is vital military forces stake their ground where the most concentrated population of people is located in order to have the greatest impact on the political, social, and economic direction of the country.[68]

Dr. John Mackinlay, a 20-year British Army officer and contemporary counterinsurgency theorist, made a significant contribution to counterinsurgency theory with the publication of his book, *The Insurgent Archipelago,* in 2009. Mackinlay believes the world has entered a new era of insurgency, a post-Maoist world. Globalization and technology have mingled to form a breeding ground for subversion and insurgent mobilization. MacKinlay describes four factors that have changed over the past three decades and contributed to a new global environment. "Transport technology; the proliferation of information and communications technology; the deregulation of the international economy; and the consequences of exposure to foreign cultures."[69] These factors set the conditions for a whole new breed of insurgent revolution in the world.

Al Qaeda is a good example of the post-Maoist insurgency that Dr. Mackinlay describes. The changing world environment facilitated Al Qaeda to recruit on a globalized scale. As the global economy and media increased in scale, access and capacity, citizens of the poorest countries began to see images and feel the influence of the rich Western countries as never before. For many, it was the first time they had been exposed to the vast economic and cultural divide that exists between the west and their own countries. The situation afforded insurgent groups such as Al Qaeda a new platform from which to spread their ideology providing "a universally relevant message or a narrative of their circumstances that had trans-national resonance."[70] Finally, the global media facilitated the effectiveness of another recruiting technique, the propaganda of the Deed. Mackinlay defines it as "the incitement of an animated or potentially violent audience through dramatic actions, rather than words."[71] There is no better example than the image of the World Trade Center collapsing on September 11th, 2001.

The global insurgency of which Mackinlay warns shares traits with the traditional Maoist insurgency he purports we have surpassed. The primary difference is the global scale and potential difficulty for the counterinsurgent force to respond, especially if the insurgency exists in many different regions. Nevertheless, the insurgency still has an overall political objective and set of grievances that the counterinsurgent force has no choice but to address. Mackinlay believes the US and UK will be forced to approach insurgency much differently in the future as technology continues to evolve and societal globalization proliferates.

It [the US and UK] will have to address insurgency as political violence and not as a form of warfare in which the military have primacy; the principles and procedures it suggests therefore have to include an array of government departments and non-government agencies which are also involved...future operations will have to engage disaffection on the ground at a very local level. The emerging theme would be that local beats global.[72]

Mackinlay conceptualizes a radically different operating environment in the future when combating insurgencies with this statement. Ironically, it is the same course of action the contemporary theorists purport, only on a widely distributed scale. A nation state that wants to counter an insurgency, in this case a global one, must utilize all elements of its national power in unison - political, diplomatic, economic, developmental, social, psychological, and military - to achieve the unity of purpose necessary to make progress, reach a settlement, or win. "The insurgent's art is to take advantage of an environment to exploit a society's aspirations and the way it exists. The counter operation organized by the state needs to be as socially astute as the insurgent's."[73]

Mackinlay does not believe Western states have reacted to the global insurgency appropriately. He suggests that the West is wedded to past solutions in countering insurgencies and as a result, has responded inappropriately to the contemporary global insurgency because the characteristics and nature has changed. Mackinlay purports the future and response to insurgency will be vastly different than it is today. "It might be possible to anticipate a future era beset by rapidly evolving forms of globalized insurgency but nevertheless contained by governments and their security forces that have successfully transitioned into the twenty-first century and are now able to exploit its information dimension and are able to engage its social characteristics."[74]

The French Counterinsurgency Camp

The French, as with the British, have had a wealth of experience with counterinsurgency operations since the end of World War II. The two most notable campaigns concerning counterinsurgency within the French experience were in Vietnam and Algeria as France jockeyed to maintain its declining empire.[75] The two campaigns lasted sixteen years sequentially, from 1946-1962, and have provided extremely valuable lessons for counterinsurgents since. Professor Douglas Porch, a military historian and professor at the Naval Postgraduate School states that the French lost the two campaigns because "its strategy was overly militarized, and its insurgent enemies produced a more compelling political scenario."[76] Most recently the French have participated in counterinsurgency operations in Afghanistan as a coalition member under the International Security and Assistance Force (ISAF).

Roger Trinquier, a French Army Officer who served in both Algeria and Vietnam, is a counterinsurgency theorist and practitioner most recognized for his book, *Modern Warfare,* originally published in 1964.

Through Trinquier's experience in Algeria, he asserts a new type of warfare, modern warfare, has emerged since World War II. He believes the future of warfare will not include two armies meeting each other on the field of battle with one emerging the victor. He states that "Warfare is now an interlocking system of actions – political, economic, psychological, and military – that aims at the overthrow of the established authority in a country and its replacement by another regime.[77] This new environment has changed the role of the military and urgently necessitated the intervening state to apply all the elements of national power against the insurgency. "Military operations, as combat actions carried out against opposing armed forces, are of only limited importance and are never the total conflict."[78] A sound counterinsurgency strategy requires unity of effort within each governmental department at all levels, National, Provincial, District, and local to adequately address the insurgency.

Trinquier recommends concentrating counterinsurgent forces in the most dense population areas that have the greatest impact on economic, development, and social progress of the country or area involved. He, consistent with every other theorist reviewed in this chapter, understood that the local population's support, voluntary or forced, is the foundation for success in a counterinsurgency. Trinquier describes how to organize forces at the local level focusing on policing, intelligence, and the local political environment. He asserts the "most desirable objective is the destruction of the politico-military organization in the intermediate areas.[79] The government and its military forces cannot allow the insurgency to control the local governmental and political situations in the cities. It must break this cycle to have a chance at gaining control and support of the population.

Trinquier's theory on modern warfare is controversial in the United States, and most other western countries, including France, because he makes a case for the necessity of torture in war. Trinquier experienced *some* tactical success in the Algerian campaign following the application of torture to gain intelligence from captured insurgents. He believes the ends justify the means when it comes to torture.

No lawyer is present for such an interrogation. If the prisoner gives the information requested, the examination is quickly terminated; in not, specialists must force his secret from him. Then as a soldier, he must face the suffering, and perhaps the death, he has heretofore managed to avoid… Once the interrogation is finished, however, the terrorist can take his place among soldiers. From then on, he is a prisoner of war like any other.[80]

Though most disagree with Trinquier on the torture issue, counterinsurgent practitioners should study his efforts and theory in all other aspects. Trinquier recognizes a critical problem with the French government and military as he believed it had not adapted itself organizationally to face the modern battlefield, and in the author's opinion, cannot approach a counterinsurgency fight as business as usual. This type of war necessitates a different strategy, a different organization and approach. Trinquier states "Will we in modern warfare make use of all necessary resources to win, as we have always done in the traditional wars of the past?"[81] Counterinsurgency strategy demands change and cannot be left solely to the military; it requires a concerted, combined approach from the intervening government and civilian agencies down to the lowest-ranking soldier on the ground.

David Galula, also a French Army officer and counterinsurgency theorist served as a tactical level commander in Algeria and an observer in Greece. Galula is best known for his book, *Counterinsurgency Warfare,* published in 1964.[82] Galula is another of the theorists who believes the population's support and the political process are inextricably bound to the counterinsurgent force's success or failure. Galula states "so intricate is the interplay between the political and the military actions that they cannot be tidily separated; on the contrary, every military move has to be weighed with regard to its political effects, and vice versa."[83] Galula also shares the common belief that countering an insurgency requires far more than purely military action. It must include psychological operations, civic and social programs, and local governance initiatives.

Galula offers four laws applicable to the counterinsurgency campaigns in which he has participated. The first law states "The support of the population is as necessary for the counterinsurgent as for the insurgent."[84] It has been a common theme thus far that when a counterinsurgent force enters a local area after an insurgency has begun, it is immediately disadvantaged because the insurgency has established popular support in the area and created grass roots governance. Even so, it is not possible to clear an area of insurgent forces and their associated political constructs with military force alone. The government must expend a considerable amount of effort to regain local support, even if it is only passive support, because usually there are not enough counterinsurgent forces to hold all of the cleared areas. All elements of the government's national power including economic, social, psychological, security, developmental, and governance, have to be applied to protect the population, gain their support, and facilitate the continued expansion of the military as it clears additional areas.

The second law states that "support is gained through an active minority."[85] Here, Galula describes the same conventional wisdom that exists in today's US Army. The basic idea is that there is a slice of the population at the local level supportive of government intervention, the loyalists. The majority of the population qualifies as fence sitters, falling somewhere in the middle, carefully weighing options to determine which side has the most to offer. The fence sitters make decisions on where to lend support based upon individual and family circumstances. The final slice of the population actively supports the insurgency, the rebels. The goal of the counterinsurgency force in this case is to leverage the loyalists to influence the active majority of fence sitters. This effort is completed while actively seeking out the rebels. Galula describes victory as "the permanent isolation of the insurgent from the population, isolation not enforced upon the population but maintained by and with the population."[86]

The third law Galula applies is that "support from the population is conditional."[87] It would be impossible to identify the slice of the population that supports the government, i.e., the counterinsurgent force, if the insurgency actively threatens that population. The counterinsurgent force must convince the local people that the insurgency can no longer harm them. This may require the counterinsurgent force to destroy a large element, or all of the insurgency, or it may mean the counterinsurgent force lives among the local people. Galula states "when a man's life is at stake, it takes more than propaganda to budge him…Political, social, economic, and other reforms, however much they ought to be wanted and popular, are inoperative when offered while the insurgent still controls the population."[88]

The fourth law states the "intensity of efforts and vastness of means are essential."[89] The counterinsurgency force must portray itself as the preferable choice. Since most locals sit the fence, swaying under the dilemma of who to support, the counterinsurgent forces have to make an immediate positive impact on the local area. This is where Galula, and all of the other counterinsurgent theorists reviewed agree. The government must inject the local area with economic, governmental, political, civic, and social programs so that the average citizen witnesses tangible positive change. The government must step up here to convince the local population that life is better under government control. The insurgents do not have the capability or resources to even fathom introducing programs into the local community on the scale governments can. The government and military must work in unison to win the day.

Galula offers a framework for countering an insurgency based upon his four rules. He clearly states there is no way the framework could be used as a cookie cutter solution or applied anywhere in the same sequential manner. Finally, Galula leaves us with the following advice on counterinsurgency. "Build (or rebuild) a political machine from the population upward."[90] This has to occur with the full support of the government and under the security of the counterinsurgent force and interventionist power.

Table 3. Strategy for Countering an Insurgency In a Selected Area

1) Concentrate enough armed forces to destroy or to expel the main body of armed insurgents.

2) Detach for the area sufficient troops to oppose an insurgent's comeback in strength, install these troops in the hamlets, villages, and towns where the population lives.

3) Establish contact with the population, control its movements in order to cut off its links with the guerrillas.

4) Destroy the local insurgent political organization.

5) Set up, by means of elections, new provisional local authorities.

6) Test these authorities by assigning them various concrete tasks. Replace the softs and the incompetents; give full support to the active leaders. Organize self-defense units.

7) Group and educate the leaders in a national political movement.

8) Win over or suppress the last insurgent remnants.

Source: David Galula, *Counterinsurgency Warfare: Theory and Practice* (Westport, CT: Praeger Security International, 2006), 55-56.

The US and Australian Counterinsurgency Camp

A large volume of counterinsurgency lessons and history has been written detailing the United States Army's recent COIN campaigns including the Philippines, 1899-1902, Vietnam,1965-1975, and both Afghanistan and Iraq from 2001 and 2003 to present, respectively.[91] As the US nears the completion of a decade of conflict in Afghanistan, the war takes its place as the longest in American history. The Australians have experience in a number of counterinsurgency campaigns including Vietnam and East Timor while fighting the Afghanistan and Iraq wars alongside the United States.

John McCuen is an American counterinsurgency theorist and the author of *The Art of Counter-Revolutionary War*. He wrote the book in 1966 as the US was increasing its commitment and presence in Vietnam. McCuen aimed "to stress the political, psychological, and military fundamentals and develop a set of guiding principles which can be used to understand and conduct this new type of warfare."[92] When discussing the principles of counter-revolutionary war, McCuen contends they are the mirror image of revolutionary principles. In short the principles are the same, aimed at destroying the enemy while securing the support of the local population. The problem for the counterinsurgent force is that it usually comes into this process late and has to first determine where the insurgency stands in the process before it can create a strategy to interdict the insurgency.

Table 4. Strategic Principles of revolutionary and counter-revolutionary warfare.

1) Preserving Oneself and Annihilating the Enemy.

2) Establishing Strategic Bases.

3) Mobilizing the Masses.

4) Seeking Outside Support.

5) Unifying the Effort.

Source: John McCuen, *The Art of Counter-Revolutionary War* (Harrisburg, PA: Stackpole Books, 1966), 73.

McCuen points to the organization of governance at all levels while focusing government resources on the local area to counter the existing insurgent organization. He cites this as "the vital first step in the governing power's strategy to thwart revolutionary attempts to control the population."[93] McCuen also points to the importance of raising local police or security forces to protect local areas. The counterinsurgent force will never be large enough to protect these areas from recurring insurgent influence. Once the local areas are secure and the people trust the counterinsurgency is there to stay, the government introduces measures and begins to change the environment for the better.[94]

McCuen warns that western governments have the tools to win the counter-revolutionary fight but they have a difficult time adapting their rigid structures and selecting the right tools for the fight. McCuen states "Inherent in this process is early recognition of the nature of the revolutionary threat and application of a maximum psycho-politico-military effort in time to seize the initiative."[95] The process involves the military and the government working in concert to bring all assets to bear either sequentially or simultaneously, depending on the situation. The government must commit to the cause from the beginning and understand there is no quick victory when fighting an insurgency. If the government is not committed to a possible protracted campaign, it should not go to war. McCuen warns of this as clearly and concisely as possible when he states "half-measures lead only to protracted, costly defeats."[96]

David Kilcullen, an Australian Army Officer and contemporary counterinsurgency theorist conducted counterinsurgency operations with the Australian Army in East Timor in 1999 and participated in peace enforcement operations in both Cyprus and Bougainville in the 1990s. Most recently, Kilcullen served as an advisor to General Petraeus in Iraq and is best known for his two books, *The Accidental Guerrilla,* published in 2009, and *Counterinsurgency,* published in 2010. Kilcullen has the innate ability to turn theory into a workable, practical framework that is equally palatable and accessible to all ranks.

In Kilcullen's book, *The Accidental Guerrilla,* he offers a framework that describes how locals are recruited, in many cases this happens purely by accident, as a direct result of the conflict between the insurgent and counter-insurgent forces. Kilcullen describes the process in four phases: "Infection, Contagion, Intervention, and Rejection."[97] Kilcullen uses Al Qaeda in his example of the process; however, it applies to a general insurgency regardless of its affiliation as well. In the infection stage the insurgency inserts itself into a local region and establishes a base area from which it will begin its operations. The insurgency begins to influence the local population using both soft and hard tactics, infiltrates local governance, and uses psychological operations to establish its political or ideological beliefs.[98]

In the contagion phase, the insurgency begins to expand its influence from its base area to the surrounding villages, districts, regions or provinces. The insurgency leverages propaganda to spread its political beliefs and ideology to influence surrounding communities and uses violence if necessary to eliminate local authority figures unwilling to cooperate. The insurgency expands its influence within local governance and establishes new systems to facilitate its political and ideological beliefs. Kilcullen cites the contagion phase as the "critical stage in the process, since without it the terrorist presence in a given area would be unlikely to attract international attention or to present a threat to the world community at large, hence the next state (intervention) would not occur."[99] It is at this stage that the government realizes it has a problem and must act. As many of the previous theorists have identified, the government reacts after the insurgency has implanted its political or ideological beliefs into local society.

The intervention stage occurs when the government or counterinsurgent force responds to the insurgent contagion of society. The government, usually armed with a powerful military, moves in to destroy the insurgency and restore society to its pre-insurgent ways. The counterinsurgent force fights the insurgency fiercely and may capture or eliminate a large number of them. In the process, the counterinsurgent force has probably made a number of mistakes in its pursuit of the insurgency, incurring a number of civilian casualties, destroying property, houses, crops, vehicles, or equipment. The locals in the area, who likely never considered fighting before, are placed in a position to take a side. Each individual must make a rational decision based on his or her personal situation. "The terrorists may have been seen as outsiders until this point, their identity as such has been not fixed but 'contingent': as soon as the foreigners or infidels appear in the area, by comparison the terrorists are able to paint themselves as relative locals and opportunistically draw on local loyalties for support."[100]

The rejection phase occurs as the local people decide who to support. These decisions feature a number of components. Who will win the conflict? Who will be here when the conflict is over? What does each side offer me individually or for my family? Kilcullen states "this is the phase in which the local people begin to become accidental guerrillas."[101] The locals who choose the insurgency do not fight with them because they necessarily share the same rigid ideology or political aspirations; they do it because it was the most logical choice for them personally. Regardless, the cycle shows that for the locals trapped inside this stressful process of conflict between the insurgent and counterinsurgent forces, good people who never envisioned themselves as guerrillas can become insurgents overnight. All it takes is the loss of property, family, or friend amid the stress and chaos and suddenly the cause has become personal.[102]

Kilcullen, such as Galula before him, recognizes the potential assets that government or counterinsurgent forces have at their disposal. In Kilcullen's view, if a counterinsurgent force can break through this aforementioned process, protect the population, and implement immediate government measures, political, economic, social, and psychological, that produce tangible benefits to the local population, the counterinsurgent force has a solid chance at success. Kilcullen states "victory does not demand that we reduce violence to zero or establish peace and prosperity in absolute terms. It only demands that we return the system to what is normal – for that society, in that region."[103]

30

How theorists would react to the Population versus Enemy Centric Debate

The theorists would dismiss the current debate between population and enemy-centric counterinsurgency immediately, calling it irrelevant. Each theorist, regardless of background or pedigree, agrees that war serves a political purpose. Not one of the theorists identified a silver bullet approach to counterinsurgency methods or war. Each asserts we must implement all elements of power available and be savvy enough to apply those elements when the situation warrants it. Popular and political support of the people is critical to success. The theorists would never dismiss a resource that could help them win or achieve a political compromise. Nor would they try only to eliminate the enemy, which is the thrust of the enemy-centric camp. Limiting focus to a singular strategy is unwise and counterproductive. War is war to these theorists, no matter how big or small. A balanced approach, utilizing all elements of national power and considering the application of every available resource within the strategy is critical to success.

Notes

1.   Sir General Frank Kitson was a British Officer, and commonly referred to as a classical Counterinsurgency theorist, that conducted Counterinsurgency operations in Kenya, Malaya, Cyprus, and Northern Ireland. He is the author of numerous books to include *Bunch of Five*, detailing his experience in Kenya, Malaya, and Cyprus, and *Low Intensity Operations,* which establishes a framework for Counterinsurgents and details in general, the best practices of Counterinsurgency at the local level as he experienced them throughout his distinguished career.

2.   Frank Kitson, *Low Intensity Operations: Subversion, Insurgency, and Peacekeeping* (St. Petersburg, FL: Hailer Publishing, 2009), 3

3.   It is important to note that all wars have irregular and asymmetric characteristics and components, not just counterinsurgency campaigns. In this context, the author is showing that while vast divisions between groups can easily fuel subversion and insurgency, there is often 5 degrees of separation between the strategies each, the insurgent and the counterinsurgent, must adopt to attain their objectives or force political settlement or compromise. A couple common factors are almost always the active and passive support of the population and the right to govern nationally or in specific territories in the case of regional insurgencies.

4.   Two examples of regional insurgencies include the Dhofar Province of Oman discussed in detail in chapter 4 and Eastern Nuristan, Afghanistan today. The districts of Eastern Nuristan Province including Kamdesh and Barge Matal had no desire to topple the government of Afghanistan, they simply wanted the government to stay out of their area and business. Coexistence within the boundaries of Afghanistan coupled with an unwritten but understood autonomy separate of the government was perfectly acceptable to the traditional leaders in Eastern Nuristan and still is today.

5.   David Kilcullen served 20 years in the Australian Army with experience conducting counterinsurgency operations in both Cyprus and Bougainville. He is considered a modern Counterinsurgency theorist who had played a significant role in advising US and Australian Forces over the last decade during the conflicts in Iraq and Afghanistan.

6.   David Kilcullen, *Counterinsurgency* (United Kingdom: Oxford University Press, 2010), 1.

7.   Sun Tzu, *The Art of War* (London: Oxford University Press, 1963), 39.

8.   Sun Tzu.

9.   Sun Tzu.

10.   Sun Tzu., 40.

11.   Baron De Jomini, *The Art of War* (El Paso, TX: El Paso Norte Press, 2005), 66.

12. Martin Van Creveld, *The Art of War: War and Military Thought* (Washington, DC: Smithsonian Books, 2005), 220.

13. Jomini, *The Art of War*, 91.

14. Jomini, 38-39.

15. The critical point here is that counterinsurgency is war and the process to go to war is similar regardless of scale. The same process that goes into planning a conventional war against another state occurs when planning to combat an insurgency. Jomini describes the importance of analyzing every aspect of the enemy state from their people to their capabilities to their political objectives. He also describes the importance of establishing your own clear political objectives that are nested with the military strategy before proceeding going to war against another state. Although an insurgency is not a state, the same calculus is applied when making the decision to go to war against one.

16. Jomini, 35.

17. Jomini, 35-36.

18. Carl Von Clausewitz, *On War* (Princeton, NJ: Princeton University Press, 1976), 605.

19. Von Clausewitz, 480.

20. Von Clausewitz, 140.

21. Von Clausewitz, 479.

22. Von Clausewitz, 482.

23. Von Clausewitz, 480.

24. Von Clausewitz, 585.

25. Sun Tzu, *The Art of War,* 101.

26. Jomini, The Art of War, 13.

27. Clausewitz, *On War,* 479.

28. John Shy and Thomas Collier, "Revolutionary War," in *Makers of Modern Strategy,* ed. Peter Paret et al. (Princeton, NJ: Princeton University Press, 1986), 816.

29. John Mackinlay, *The Insurgent Archipelago* (London: Hurst and Company Publishers, 2009), 27.

30. Shy and Collier, "Revolutionary War," 846.

31. The Oxford dictionary of philosophy, 2008, defines Maoism as "the transposition of the theory and practice of Marxism to apply to the conditions not of the urban proletariat, but of the Chinese peasantry. In some quarters in the West, especially during the late 1960s, it became optimistically regarded as the ultimate egalitarian and communitarian political ideal.

32. Martin Van Creveld, *The Art of War,* 209.

33. Mao Tse-Tung, *On Guerrilla Warfare* (New York: Praegar Publishers, 1961), 92.

34. Tse-Tung, 89.

35. Tse-Tung, 43.

36. Robert O'Neill, *General Giap: Politician and Strategist* (New York: Praegar Publishers, 1969), 23.

37. Ho Chi Mihn was Vietnamese leader who served as prime minister between 1946 and 1955 and as president from1945 to 1969 of the Democratic Republic of North Vietnam. He was critical in starting the political party of the Democratic Republic of Vietnam and was an influential leader of the Viet Cong during Vietnam.

38. John Colvin, *Giap: Volcano Under Snow* (New York: Soho Press, Inc. 1996), 142.

39. O'Neill, *General Giap: Politician and Strategist*, 203-204.

40. Colvin, *Giap: Volcano Under Snow*, 231.

41. Colvin.

42. O'Neill, General Giap: Politician and Strategist, 204-206.

43. O'Neill, 198.

44. Andrew Birtle, *US Army Counterinsurgency and Contingency Operations Doctrine 1942-1976* (Washington, D.C: Center of Military History United States Army, 2007), 366-367.

45. O'Neill, *General Giap: Politician and Strategist*, 198..

46. Command and General Staff College Scholars Program 2011. *Scholars Program Counterinsurgency Research Study 2011.* (Fort Leavenworth, Kansas: Ike Skelton Chair in Counterinsurgency, 2010), 4 February, 2011.

47. Julian Paget, *Counter-Insurgency Operations* (New York: Walker and Company, 1967), 17.

48. Frank Kitson, *Bunch of Five* (London: Faber and Faber Limited, 1977), xi.

49. Kitson, 284.

50. Kitson, 282.

51. Kitson, 286.

52. Kitson, Low Intensity Operations, 180.

53. Kitson, 96.

54. Kitson, *Bunch of Five,* 287-288.

55. Kitson, 289.

56. Kitson, Low Intensity Operations, 200.

57. Robert Thompson, *Defeating Communist Insurgency* (St. Petersburg, FL: Hailer Publishing, 2005), 21.

58. Kitson, 21.

59. Kitson, 50-51.

60. Kitson, 63.

61. Kitson, 52.

62. Kitson, 53.

63. Kitson, 55.

64. Kitson

65. Kitson, 55.

66. Paget, Counter-Insurgency Operations, 168-170.

67. Thompson, *Defeating Communist Insurgency*, 57.

68. Paget, Counter-Insurgency Operations, 170-171.

69. Mackinlay, *The Insurgent Archipelago*, 29.

70. Mackinlay, 41.

71. Mackinlay, 124.

72. Mackinlay, 231.

73. Mackinlay, 6.

74. Mackinlay., 232.

75.   The French fought in Vietnam from 1946 to 1954 when the French ended their colonial administration and dissolved their Indo-China holdings. Algeria fought a bloody insurgency against the French from 1954 to 1962 when it attained its independence.

76. Douglas Porch, "French Imperial Warfare," in *Counterinsurgency in Modern Warfare,* ed. Daniel Marston et al. (Oxford: Osprey Publishing, 2008), 91.

77. Roger Trinquier, *Modern Warfare: A French View of Counterinsurgency* (Westport CT: Praeger Security International, 2006), 5.

78. Trinquier.

79. Trinquier, 60.

80. Trinquier, 19.

81. Trinquier, 90.

82. Galula also published an insightful book on the Algerian War titled, Pacification of Algeria: 1956-1958.

83. David Galula, *Counterinsurgency Warfare: Theory and Practice* (Westport, CT: Praegar Security International, 2006), 5.

84. Galula, 52.

85. Galula, 53.

86. Galula, 54

87. Galula.

88. Galula, 55

89. Galula.

90. Galula, 95.

91. The conflict in the Philippines would begin in 1898 and conclude in 1954. The American counterinsurgency campaign referenced in the text was a phase of the total conflict from 1899-1902.

92. John McCuen, *The Art of Counter-Revolutionary Warfare* (Harrisburg, PA: Stackpole Books, 1972), 19.

93. McCuen, 25.

94. McCuen, 182-183.

95. McCuen, 324.

96. McCuen, 330.

97. David Kilcullen, *The Accidental Guerrilla* (Oxford: Oxford University Press, 2009), 35.

98. Kilcullen, 113.

99. Kilcullen, 36.

100. Kilcullen, 38.

101. Kilcullen

102. Kilcullen, 36-37.

103. Kilcullen, Counterinsurgency, 216.

Chapter 3
Malaya: 1948 to 1960

There should be a proper balance between the military and the civil effort, with complete coordination in all fields. Otherwise a situation will arise in which military operations produce no lasting results because they are unsupported by civil follow-up action. Similarly, civilian measures, particularly in areas disputed with the insurgents, are a waste of time and money if they are unsupported by military operations to provide the necessary protection.

— Sir Robert Thompson,
Defeating Communist Insurgencies

This chapter will analyze and review strategy application within the Malayan counterinsurgency campaign. The chapter will focus on how the government and associated counterinsurgent forces administered political, military, social, economic, and psychological aspects of strategy against the insurgency. This chapter provides further evidence that there is no such thing as a purely 'soft' or 'hard' strategy, or what many US military leaders describe today as either a population-centric or an enemy-centric strategy. Even though US military circles consider the Malayan campaign a population-centric one, the evidence suggests the government applied *all* elements of national power: both an offensive kill and capture effort and a non-lethal effort, to achieving a positive outcome. In some cases, *soft* power elements were engaged too late, in others the mix of soft and hard power was skewed detrimentally in one direction or the other. For certain, this is a delicate dance in which governments must execute a carefully nuanced approach to achieve an acceptable outcome.

The Malaya Emergency

The most important single lesson that can be learned from the Malayan Emergency is that at the level of governmental decision making a very fine balance must be struck between policies directed at destroying the organizational strength of the Communists and policies aimed at creating a stable political process in the society. . . The government must be prepared to apply all its powers of coercion against the organizational basis of Communist power; but it must also seek to create the conditions which will expand the area of open political participation on the part of the public.[1]

The Malaya Emergency (1948-1960) serves as a prime example of the flexibility required by a government mired in a protracted counterinsurgency campaign. The British declared a state of emergency, including the introduction of emergency regulations, after continued escalation with the Malayan Communist Party reached a boiling point with the murder of three prominent British citizens working as farmers on June 16, 1948.[2] The emergency regulations enacted by the British government adapted the existing criminal law to facilitate swift action and justice against the insurgency. The regulations were tough and gave the British and Malay government the authority to execute preventative detention of suspected insurgents without having a trial.[3] This served as a powerful deterrent measure against the already powerful communist insurgency. "The Malayan Communist's Party's (MCP) armed wing, the Malayan Races Liberation Army (MRLA), and its support organization, the Min Yuen, sought to overthrow the British colonial administration and later, after independence in 1957, the Malayan government."[4] The goal of the Malayan Communist Party was to establish a "communist-controlled peoples' republic"[5] in Malaya.

The Malayan Communist Party originates from the Malayan People's Anti-Japanese Army (MPAJA), which had fought fiercely as a resistance movement against the Japanese during Japanese occupation.[6] Interestingly enough, the British mentored this force to fight the Japanese. The British did not guess they would face the very group they armed in a protracted counterinsurgency campaign three short years later.[7] Once the MPAJA and British defeated the Japanese in 1945, the British returned to the region to reclaim their colonial holding. This did not sit well with the MPAJA as they found the British undeserving to regain control over the land that they had just fought for.[8]

The Malayan Communist Party had every intension of taking over the country in the wake of the Japanese withdrawal, but the end of the War came suddenly before their plans were complete and the British were able to re-establish their position, disbanding the Mayalan Peoples Anti Japanese Army with expressions of goodwill, supplemented by gratuities and an appropriate issue of honors and awards.[9]

Once the MPAJA was officially disbanded by the British, the MCP quickly took their place as a legal entity to represent the Communist Chinese in Malaya.

Over the next three years the Malayan Communist Party grew increasingly effective organizing violence against the British run government. Their aim was to damage the economy fueled by tin mines and the numerous rubber plantations and saturate trade and labor union membership.[10] The MCP organized significant attacks that disrupted industrial capacity. "In 1947 there were 291 strikes [against mines and rubber plantations], involving 69,000 men and the loss of nearly 700,000 man-days."[11] The MCP did not stop there. They also targeted prominent local leaders working with the British, killing a couple hundred between 1945 and 1948.[12]

The British counterinsurgency strategy in Malaya evolved significantly to counter the threat of the Malayan Communist Party. The British strategy initially deployed battalion and brigade sized units to conduct search and destroy techniques against the insurgency. This was initiated by Major General C.H. Boucher between 1948 and 1950.[13] Although the conduct of large scale unit sized operations was conventional wisdom at the time, executing operations within a jungle setting in which the British military had little experience made the technique less than effective. In order to address the lack of jungle experience, the British gathered leaders with jungle expertise and formed a training center. British leaders deployed from England were required to receive 167 hours of training in jungle warfare techniques. Large scale search and destroy operations were re-evaluated and some smaller scale units were formed, such as the Ferret force, with success.[14]

The counterinsurgency strategy began to shift between1950-1952 as the collective experience and ability of soldiers at the tactical level to operate in the jungle increased. Lieutenant General Harold Briggs arrived as Director of Operations in 1950 fueling a more balanced strategy. The Briggs Plan increased the focus on population protection and control while maintaining an offensive, aggressive disposition against the insurgency.[15] Large scale offensive operations were replaced with smaller, lethal, intelligence driven operations against the insurgency. After an assessment of the situation in 1952, Lieutenant General Harold Templer took control between 1952 and 1954. Unlike Briggs, Templer took control as both the Director of Operation and the High Commissioner. This authority allowed him to further unify the effort.[16] Templer maintained Briggs balanced framework while adapting and improving it to increase the pressure on the insurgency forcing them into significant decline by the time he left in 1954. From 1954 to 1957, the British worked to transfer power to the Malayan government and finally, from 1957 to the conclusion of the insurgency in 1960, the Malay government worked to reach a settlement with their indigenous Chinese population by further including them in the political, social, economic, and security aspects of Malay society.[17]

Throughout counterinsurgency campaigns in history, one of the most common government miscalculations is failing to recognize the threat and rising power of a subversive element within its ranks before it has developed into a powerful foe, capable of challenging the government's authority politically, socially, and militarily.[18] Sir Robert Thompson warns of this stating "any sensible government should attempt to defeat an insurgency movement during the subversive build-up phase. . . prevention is better than cure, and the government must be positive in its approach."[19] In the case of Malaya, the British government had supported the MCP during their struggle against the Japanese from 1941-1945, but failed to recognize how quickly it was growing disenfranchised. By 1948 negotiations with the British had broken down, union regulations were in place working against the MCP, and deportation sharply rose.[20] The British understood the MCP was an emerging threat; however, they underestimated the military scale of the MRLA and the social and political potential and momentum they would generate in Malay society.[21] By the time the British declared the situation in Malaya an emergency in 1948, the insurgency had around 2000 members.[22] "The British problem was not one of a lack of information [on the MRLA] rather, the difficulty was one of interpretation and of choice of policies to meet the possible threat."[23]

At the emergency's outset, the British chose to counter the MRLA threat largely through a legalistic approach "construing the Emergency to be essentially a problem of re-establishing law and order...Once the government had established its objective to be the elimination of lawlessness, it could neither compromise with itself nor permit the general public to expect a compromise with the MCP."[24] The civil administration's inability to efficiently organize and coordinate efforts within the individual government departments countering the MCP complicated matters. There was confusion as to which department was responsible for which function in relation to the insurgency and support for the counterinsurgency effort. The Government struggled to establish clear guidelines and priorities when appropriating resources to its departments and overall counterinsurgency effort.[25] The government response to the emergency moved forward; however, it was often disjointed as individual departments did their best to contribute to the effort but often overlapped resources and wasted energy because they were making decisions in isolation.

The government utilized the Malayan police force in its effort to restore law and order by amplifying its size by 30,000 between 1948 and 1951.[26] "The 30,000 additional police, known as special constables, were not regular police, trained in routine law enforcement and apprehension of criminals, but paramilitary forces whose sole purpose was to carry out counterinsurgency and infantry operations."[27] The military's role was subordinate to police efforts and was largely used to support police operations.[28] The military's strategy to defeat the insurgency between 1948 and 1951 was heavy-handed and often counter-productive as it frequently inflicted a heavy civilian casualty rate as an effect of operations.[29] The army was organized to conduct large offensive operations intended to kill or capture Communist insurgents in droves.[30] The conventional approach was commonplace to the British as they had used it to destroy German formations in Europe just years before.[31]

One Malay veteran described this approach as "bait bashing."[32] Bait bashing is a short-term strike operations, usually lasting 24-48 hours, originating from one's combat outpost with the goal of killing or capturing insurgents. Once the unit reaches the location where the insurgents are expected, they conduct intrusive searches of the area.

The soldiers would kick everything out, including woman and children, [and] mine detectors around to see if they could find any arms. If we didn't find anything, then we'd say let's be nice. "We've got a doctor here; he can give you some medical help." You think that is going to turn them onto your side? You've alienated their people. They will hate you. And then you go back down the hill again [back to your combat outpost], what I call mowing the grass. You've achieved nothing.[33]

The massive, short-term British strike operations usually failed to ferret out insurgency pockets. The strategy against the MRLA was one of counter-terror and had mixed results. While some short term success was present in dismantling larger MRLA groups and increasing intelligence as a result of detention, the death toll on civilians fueled MRLA recruiting. The MRLA quickly broke up into smaller groups to preserve their forces and increase the effectiveness of their attacks. The British Army continued its large-scale operations to hunt down the insurgency but the insurgents were successful in avoiding extensive contact with the government forces.[34]

Although the insurgents suffered significant casualties upon confronting government forces, they managed to expand their active base to "nearly 8,000 by the end of 1951, with 10,000 – 15,000 regular workers in the Min Yuen."[35] As the MRLA and Min Yuen gained traction and popular support within the local communities, it was clear only a significant change in strategy could reverse the MCP's momentum. The Malayan veteran said he came to accept one undeniable truth about bait bashing operations, drawn from all the counterinsurgency campaigns of his career. If your operation against the insurgency achieves "a short term success, but doesn't affect long term aim, it's a failure."[36]

The British experienced plenty of short term success against the MRLA from 1948-1950 as they learned pivotal lessons on how to deal with the insurgency and operate in the jungle at the company level.[37] The strategy focused effort on killing or capturing the enemy via large formations and crushing firepower, an enemy-centric approach, while failing to appropriately deploy other essential resources both against the insurgency and in support of the population. This strategy was also referred to as a counter-terror approach using large scale sweep operations to find, fix, and destroy the enemy.[38] Slowly the British realized they could not kill their way to victory in Malaya. The offensive mindset was good; however, the collateral damage inflicted on the local population as a result of the enemy-centric approach made recruiting for the MRLA easy and the insurgency proliferated.[39] The strategy would have to change. General Frank Kitson served in the campaign and later remarked, "it took about two years of trial and error for the Government to develop a reasonable strategy."[40]

In reaction to the worsening Malayan situation in 1950, retired Lieutenant General Sir Harold Briggs was chosen to reverse the momentum of the MRLA and restore law and order. He arrived in April, 1950 and immediately implemented changes which directly impacted unity of effort with which the Malay government had struggled with during the first two years of the emergency.[41] Still, Briggs lacked the command authority and the autonomy to run the counterinsurgency effort completely. Briggs acted not as a commander but as an "operational controller". He was tasked to organize both the counterinsurgency operations of the police and of the military.[42] Briggs immediately addressed the unity of effort between the police, military, and civil government efforts by enacting an executive committee system at all levels, the Brigg's Plan.

Police, military, and associated civil departments participated in Briggs' formalized system in which power brokers at all levels met, shared information, and discussed daily decisions as well as long-range plans. The committee system reached all the way to the top with Briggs forming and actively participating in the Federal War Council (FWC) and the Federal Joint Intelligence Advisory Committee[43]. The Federal War Council, chaired by Briggs, established policy and appropriated resources for the counterinsurgency effort against the MRLA.[44] The Joint Intelligence Advisory Committee enabled the fusion of intelligence from the army, police, and local government collecting, coordinating and analyzing information across the joint and interagency spectrum.[45] Prior to this fusion effort, each entity had its own intelligence stovepipe and had struggled to share information and intelligence across organizations. The state and district levels had similar committees called the State War Executive Committee (SWEC) and the District War Executive Committee (DWEC), respectively.[46] Although these positive changes facilitated a holistic government approach, the system was imperfect. For most decisions, each committee's consensus sufficed; however, reaching that consensus presented a challenge in the face of certain volatile issues. It was clear to Briggs that he needed command authority over all operations in Malaya. He never got it.

Briggs quickly deemed the large-scale military operations to kill or capture insurgents to be ineffective. While the MRLA suffered heavy casualties in the wake of targeted sweep operations, the process of actually locating insurgent bands was relatively unsuccessful. The MRLA was making significant progress infiltrating isolated local villages in the jungle and gaining popular support.[47] The Malayan police experienced some success at keeping MRLA and Min Yuen influence out of the accessible villages but the remote jungle settlements were much more difficult to interdict. Chinese squatters posed the most significant challenge to the security forces in the jungle. There were thousands of squatters dispersed in the jungle. Their dispersion made them easy targets for the insurgents to influence and target.[48] The MRLA had freedom of maneuver in the jungle and access to food, shelter, and support from the indigenous Chinese population who did not have the means to defend themselves.

Briggs envisioned a strategy to defeat the MRLA insurgency. One counterinsurgency theorist stated the Briggs plan "was nothing less than the Master Plan for the winning of the campaign."[49]

Table 5. The Four Main Aims of the Briggs Plan.

a) To dominate the populated areas and to build up a feeling of complete security, which would in time result in a steady and increasing flow of information coming from all sources.

b) To break up the Communist organizations within the populated areas.

c) To isolate the bandits from their food supply organizations in the populated areas.

d) To destroy the bandits by forcing them to attack the Security Forces on their own ground.

Source: Julian Paget, *Counter-Insurgency Operations* (New York: Walker and Company, 1967), 56-57.

While Briggs understood the importance of attriting the military capacity and strength of the insurgency, his plan set the stage for the British and Malay security forces to regain the initiative. No longer would the security forces conduct large-scale offensive operations and expect the insurgency to face their strength on the battlefield. "Briggs issued a tactical directive which stressed the importance of maintaining the 'framework' and of operating in small controlled units."[50] It was clear the chances of closing with and destroying the enemy favored a government force small enough to not give off a signature with each movement. The insurgency had already proven they would not disadvantage their forces by exposing them to the more powerful Malay security forces. The intricate workings of Briggs' strategy offered a more balanced approach to tackling the MRLA. The weekly meetings to fuse the civilian-military strategy better focused the government resources to work in concert and attack the insurgency from all angles.

One of the most important elements of the Briggs strategy, and one that created major problems in the beginning, was the resettlement effort to separate the insurgency from the local population and prevent them from interdicting the government-backed rubber and mining industry. Resettlement came in the following two forms: relocation and re-groupment.

Relocation, which involved the removal of dispersed rural dwellers whether squatters or legitimate settlers, to prepare fortified sites often remote from their existing homes. In some cases existing village: in others it involved the establishment of a completely new settlement; and re-groupment or regrouping, which involved the concentration and protection of estate and mine labor either within the property or close to it, with emphasis on providing security within easy access of the community's place of work.[51]

Resettlement was a highly effective method of separating the local population, especially the jungle dwelling ethnic Chinese most at risk to insurgent influence and support, from the insurgency. Locations chosen to establish resettlement camps were as easily accessible and defendable by government forces as they were difficult to attack by the insurgency.[52] As the number of 'Squatters' and jungle dwellings decreased, the insurgency's ability to sustain their forces with food and support faltered. This facilitated one the Briggs plan's main goals of attacking MCP's logistical systems and lines of communication.[53]

Resettlement was not executed without a long list of issues. Horrendous living conditions typified many of the camp experiences, despite the best British and Malay government intentions. These circumstances would be handled and improved over the years but, there was no doubt about it, population resettlement was toxic to the insurgency's vitality. By 1957, when the Malaya government was granted its independence from Britain, around "500,000 of Mayala's 1950s population of approximately 5,000,000"[54] had been resettled. The resettlement program was a top priority; it was executed very quickly with the bulk of resettlement complete by 1952. The resettlement effort proved sustainable in Malaya, considering that "of the more than 500 resettlement areas established between 1950 and 1960, only six were abandoned and resettled elsewhere, mainly on security grounds."[55]

Briggs implemented effective population controls within the resettled villages by executing curfews, establishing a food control program, strictly registering locals, and providing security to protect the population all legally under enacted "Emergency Regulations."[56] The food control program and curfews were aimed at both denying the insurgency the ability to buy food in the villages and preventing village sympathizers from supplying the insurgency. The program was marginally effective prior to resettlement as insurgents could still lean on the ethnic Chinese squatters in the jungle; however, it became an extremely powerful weapon once resettlement was completed.[57]

The system was administered by the SWECs and DWECs, which were allowed considerable local option…it involved strict rationing of certain foods at state discretion, village gate checks and curfew hours (also on roads), spot checks, careful inspection of road and rail traffic at checkpoints, mobile food-check teams, and strict accounting for all stocks and sales of specified foods and supplies. Food cans were even punctured when sold to prevent their being stored. Sales could be made only to people with ID cards, and records had to be kept for inspection in food-restricted areas.[58]

The resettlement program crippled the insurgency's ability to sustain operations. The insurgency literally had no one left to co-opt, threaten or intimidate by the time the main thrust of the resettlement effort had occurred. Life as an insurgent in the jungles of Malaya was growing increasingly difficult. Most importantly the British and Malayan security forces regained the initiative through these measures. "The Communist guerrillas had to converge on the [resettled] villages in order to obtain their necessary supplies… Instead of the Communists being able to exploit the advantages of surprise in ambush operations, it was [now] the British who were able to lay the ambushes."[59] The British and Malayan security forces could identify insurgent groups attempting to infiltrate the resettled villages and take action. It was not a perfect system as it was difficult to secure nearly 500 resettled villages. The insurgency did successfully infiltrate a number of the villages; however, the resettlement strategy still greatly favored the government.

The insurgency faced a real problem. Their sole refuge was the jungle but their logical supporters there had been removed. Only one other jungle population remained: the aborigines. Initially, many aborigine people had been resettled with the Chinese as part of the anti-insurgency campaign. The British government realized moving them meant the military had lost the valuable MRLA intelligence the aborigines had always provided, so the British returned them to their areas.[60] Jungle forts were established in an effort to deny the insurgency access to the aborigines. "Each was little more than an area hacked out of the jungle at which a police post of platoon strength [thirty men] was established, and a light aircraft strip was built."[61] The jungle forts effectively denied the insurgency access to the population while also garnering that population's support for the British military. The forts offered the aborigines basic services previously unheard of. As a Mayala veteran recalls, "What could you get at a jungle fort? You could go in and buy your axes and your sarongs, you could get medical support, it's all of those little things."[62] The jungle forts further denied the insurgency access to sanctuary areas. In the end, the only sanctuary area available to the MRLA was Thailand, and that is exactly where they went.

General Briggs launched an initiative to create an irregular security force, the Home Guard, to protect populations in both the resettled and existing villages.[63] The Home Guard enabled villagers to take responsibility for security by appointing individuals to serve on the force and protect their local population from insurgency influence. Home Guard would also free up the government's police and military for other operations.[64] The Home Guard was created for the purpose of protecting villages and establishing local security, reaching a strength of 200,000 by 1954.[65] The Home Guard concept further organized the resettled and government controlled villages making it more difficult for the insurgency to penetrate. "A headman for each village and Home Guard was to be nominated under the supervision of the District Officer. Each house in the village was to have a tenant-in-chief who would be responsible to the headman for reporting the names and movements of people in his area of the village."[66]

It is important to understand here that the Briggs strategy and framework to improve security and regain control was not immediately lauded as a success or even appreciated as a potentially effective plan. In 1951, the Briggs plan was in full swing and the resettlement initiative was moving at lightning speed but the insurgency was potent and desperate.[67] The extreme level of violence in 1951 was the highest it had been since the emergency began, accounting for "1,000 insurgents and 500 security forces killed."[68] The situation looked grim for the government security forces and to make matters worse, Sir Henry Gurney, the British High Commissioner to Malaya, was killed on 7 October 1951. Gurney's death was an absolute outrage to the British and resulted in the government calling for a renewed and tougher effort against the insurgents. They demanded increasingly robust policies and resources be applied to the counterinsurgency effort.[69] Briggs made clear that his lack of authority and decision-making power decreased his ability to prosecute the emergency. In one of his final acts as the director of operations, Briggs wrote in report how not having complete control in Malaya hobbled his efforts and made it particularly difficult to get the police in line.[70]

Briggs four part plan and efforts to reform the strategy would prove decisive in turning around the war effort in favor of the British and Malay government but it was not immediately apparent. He distanced the police and military away from the enemy-centric strategy, focusing them on a more balanced approach. While he still did not have the political autonomy he desired to run the war at maximum efficiency, he improved civilian-military unity of effort and reapportioned resources to boost government efforts and degrade the insurgency.[71] Briggs integrated intelligence collection departments and agencies within the government and military, streamlining the system. He utilized resources to implement population control measures to protect the population while denying the insurgency critical logistic support.[72] He boosted psychological operations against the insurgency by disseminating leaflets to communicate directly with the insurgents.[73] Briggs bolstered funding and training for the police, expanded the Malay military, and launched lethal kill and capture operations against the insurgency utilizing smaller, more focused, operations. Briggs established the foundation for a balanced strategy that employed available resources across the lines of effort in support of the counterinsurgency campaign.

The British Government was quick to re-examine the situation after Gurney's death, sending Oliver Lyttelton, the British Secretary of State, to make recommendations for future efforts.[74] Lyttelton devised a way ahead and plan for the Emergency after having examined the situation and extensively discussing the issues with the exiting General Briggs. General Briggs departed Malaya in November 1951, feeling he had failed to turn the tide of the war. He died in 1952, unaware that his efforts predicated a dramatic turn-around, which greatly impacted the successful conclusion of the Emergency eight years later.[75]

Table 6. Secretary of State for Colonies Oliver Lyttelton's 6 Point Malaya Strategy.

1) Need for a unified, overall direction of the civil administration and the military forces.

2) The police should be reorganized and retrained.

3) Government-run compulsory primary education was necessary to counter Communist propaganda in Communist-infiltrated schools.

4) Resettlement areas should be given a high level of protection.

5) The home guard had to be reorganized and large numbers of Malayan-Chinese enlisted.

6) The strain on an undermanned civil service had to be alleviated.

Source: Richard Stubbs, "From Search and Destroy to Hearts and Minds," In *Counterinsurgency in Modern Warfare,* ed. Daniel Marston et al. (Oxford: Osprey Publishing LTD, 2008), 108-109.

General Sir Gerald Templer was selected to take over operations in Malaya in the early months of 1952. Based on Secretary Lyttelton's assessment, coupled with General Briggs' assertion that he lacked the necessary power required to direct operations in Malaya and unify the effort across the government, General Templer was given complete control. Not only would he take over for General Briggs as the Director of Operations but he would concurrently serve as the High Commissioner. This gave General Templer total control over the military and civilian efforts in Malaya and would allow him to better organize counterinsurgency efforts against the communists.[76] Templer's near dictator like power gave him the ability to force unity of command across the government and make timely decisions that led to rapid execution. It is important to understand here that while Templer commanded the Federal government and its associated foreign policy, he only controlled one of the nine Malayan states that including the capital city. The other eight states were governed by Malayan princes who had control of the internal workings of their respective states. Templer still had to negotiate with these governors on a range of political issues.[77] Political discussion and pressure was also mounting back in Britain to grant the Malayan government independence. General Templer was directed to make that goal a key component in his strategy as he moved forward.[78]

General Templer was highly successful in Malaya but it is important to note that the critical framework for his success was established by General Briggs.[79] Templer did institute some immediate changes, refinements, and new initiatives using his authority and power that enabled the government to apply a level of unity of effort that had previously eluded them. Templer immediately merged the civilian and military decision-making bodies. He created two deputies, one for the military operations and one for civilian government operations; both answered directly to him.[80] He stated "Any idea that the business of normal civil government and the business of the Emergency are two separate entities must be killed for good and for all. The two activities are completely and utterly interrelated."[81]

The bolstered emphasis to support the Emergency by the British government gave Templer the power to request, recruit, and employ absolutely the best minds Britain had to offer. Templer understood that both the expansion and retraining of the current police force was critical so he brought in one of the best policemen Britain had to offer, Sir Arthur Young, the Commissioner of the London Metropolitan Police to fuel the effort.[82] Young executed his duties and responsibilities as advertised. He opened police training facilities across Malaya, focused the Malayanization of the leadership the number one concern, and made the most promising police instructors in police school s across the country.[83]He also understood the importance of integrating ethnic Chinese into the police force and made a major effort to do so, resulting in the addition of over 1,000 between 1952 and 1953.[84] Young also realized that the harried effort to recruit police and get them on the street in the previous years had made for a very ineffective and inefficient police force. While creating and executing the critical police training the Malayan security forces so desperately needed, Young also "reduced the force by 10,000 personnel, cutting mostly special constables who had been recruited early in the emergency and who had proven incompetent or corrupt."[85]

General Templer coined the oft-used term "Hearts and Minds" that has frequently described aspects of our military's counterinsurgency efforts in Iraq and Afghanistan. When asked how he intended to bring the Emergency in Malaya under control he stated, "The answer lies not in pouring more troops into the jungle, but rests in the hearts and minds of the Malayan people."[86] Templer demonstrated great leadership to the British and Malayan government agencies, the security forces, and the

Malayan people in reinforcing this point. He seemed to care deeply about the Malayan people and they recognized it. He listened to their grievances and created policies to support solutions when possible.

Templer strongly believed "he could win the Emergency if he could get two-thirds of the people on his side."[87] To do that, Templer had to carefully think through how to give the population, especially the Chinese population, enough confidence in themselves and their security situation to insure they would choose the government over the communist insurgents.[88] Civilian policies and directives coupled with military action were refocused with that aim in mind. Whether Templer accomplished his goal of winning Chinese hearts and minds or if the Chinese sided with the government because of the rigid population control measures may never be known.[89] Most likely, both efforts together contributed to the end result.

One of the most important things Templer was to optimize the strategy that Briggs had already laid out for him. Briggs had already created the framework that would be credited for progress, it just wasn't visible yet.[90] Templer optimized a number of already established programs. He nurtured the feeling of security and safety throughout the Malayan population by expanding the Home Guard program that had been slow to start under Briggs. "Goals were set to expand the home guard to 240,000 men and to ensure that there was proper supervision of the force by trained officers."[91] The same principles that had been applied to the regular security forces were also in effect for the Home Guard. Templer knew it was critical to include ethnic Chinese in the program. Arming the ethnic Malayan Chinese, many of whom came from the same communities as those who had joined the insurgency, was perilous business.[92]

Templer knew it was a risk to arm the indigenous Chinese but it was one worth taking and it paid off in the end. It turned out that allowing the indigenous Chinese to be both part of the Malayan government and solution trumpeted the call to communist ideology that the Min Yuen or MCP were spouting. "50,000 Chinese willingly joined the Home Guards, and by 1954, 150 Chinese villages were protected by their own security forces."[93] The well-organized training and careful expansion of Home Guard was critical to establishing sufficient force in the villages to provide locals a sense of security. In the end, the Home Guard "formed a valuable link between the Security Forces and the populace, and they provided much useful information…and freed trained troops from static duties."[94]

Templer also perceived a critical need to expand governance capacity at all levels. As the Home Guard expanded and rapidly upgraded village security situations, it was just as crucial to ensure responsive governance was in place to meet people's needs. This included immediately addressing the second and third order effects created by the resettlement effort. In the rush to accomplish the resettlement mission, many of the hastily established villages lacked the infrastructure to support appropriate living conditions. Templer recognized that the resettlement areas to which over half a million ethnic Chinese had been forcibly moved required dramatic improvement. How could one expect to gain a population's passive or active support if the resettled areas were significantly inferior to the ones left behind?

Templer ordered the resettlement centers to be called "new villages... The provision of services and amenities for the new villages was no longer to be referred to as 'after care' but as 'development.'"[95] The aim was to win the Chinese villagers' support by improving and enhancing their quality of life to the extent that the Min Yuen and MCP could no longer compete. Templer vastly expanded local governance and made a concerted effort to include ethnic Chinese in all aspects of the process, including elected positions. As local government was established in the villages, things began to get better for the local people and services that had never been available before, like water and electricity, were coming available.[96] Templer offered a huge incentive to villages and areas that successfully governed and defended themselves while shunning the insurgency and openly supporting the government. One of Templer's most influential incentives debuted "in 1953 by instituting a policy of declaring 'white areas,' from which the Emergency Regulations were lifted once insurgency in them had died down."[97] This essentially allowed villages achieving white area status to return to normalcy, or, at least, to take a huge step toward it. The incentive of village white area status proved overwhelmingly successful. The village of "Malacca was declared the first 'white area' in September 1953…By mid-1955, a third of Malaya's population lived in cleared 'white' areas."[98]

While Templer clearly understood the importance of inclusion, population empowerment, increased governance at all levels and meticulous security force training and expansion, he also pursued the insurgency tenaciously. Templer advocated a balanced approach to combating the insurgency. A critical strategy component was the use of intelligence-driven, targeted kill and capture operations to render the insurgency ineffective. Army units conducted intensive in-country jungle warfare training.[99] Commanders decreased the number of soldiers in their patrols and increased the amount of time they spent in the jungle searching for insurgents.[100] Security force and Home Guard expansions had a positive second order effect on intelligence.

The focused, intelligence driven, small unit jungle operations proved highly effective for the British. The totality of the sanctions, emergency regulations, and increasingly effective counterinsurgency focused kill and capture operations proved too much for the insurgents. The framework established by Briggs in 1950 re-focusing the counterinsurgency effort across the lines of effort and initiating effective population control measures against the insurgency between 1950 and 1952 coupled by Templer's optimization of the framework between 1952 and 1954, broke the back of the insurgency.[101] Although the effectiveness of Briggs plan would not be realized until Templer's tenure in 1952, Two-thirds of the insurgents were destroyed between 1952 and 1954.[102]

Templer maximized the effectiveness of a number of significant initiatives that directly impacted the counterinsurgency effort. His keen use of information, psychological warfare, and propaganda both, against the insurgency and to enhance public opinion, is worth mentioning. Sir Robert Thompson, a British counterinsurgency theorist who is summarized in chapter 2, explains the importance of psychological warfare.

A successful psychological warfare campaign will depend on a clear and precise government surrender policy towards the insurgents. Such a policy has three main aims: (1) to encourage insurgents to surrender; (2) to sow dissension between insurgent rank and file and their leaders; and (3) to create an image of government both to the insurgents and to the population which is both firm and efficient but at the same time just and generous.[103]

The British proved experts in their use of psychological warfare, attracting a considerable number of Surrendered Enemy Personnel (SEPs). In many cases, the SEPs could be reintegrated into Malay society, serving in the Home Guard or, in some cases, the security forces. SEPs became a crucial component of both the intelligence effort and devising the psychological warfare strategy. In a combat assessment of Operation Sword which began in September 1953, Captain D.J Wilford of the 22 Special Air Service Regiment (SAS) explains his use of propaganda in the fight. "Millions of surrender leaflets and safe conduct passes were dropped into the trees, voice aircraft broadcast daily and teams visited the surrounding areas speaking of the operation and all it meant to them."[104] Captain's Wilford's description of how propaganda was employed in Operation Sword typifies its use against the MRLA nationwide.

52

By the time Templer's command ended in 1954, significant progress had been made by the British and Malay government against the insurgency. General Templer had been the right man for the job, poring over General Briggs' framework and command confines, advocating for change, and then implementing and refining the framework successfully. More political power enabled Templer to achieve greater unity of effort than Briggs had that, in turn, created an even more balanced strategy. He had fueled the Malayanization of the government and security forces as he multiplied the number of Malays in every institution, making a point to include the indigenous Chinese. He understood, as Briggs had, the security forces were key. He redoubled efforts to train and re-train as necessary.[105] Templer revamped struggling resettlement camps into modern new villages, complete with essential services. He rewarded government controlled areas and supporters with development and economic assistance.

Templer stepped up efforts to communicate to the local people and insurgency through psychological operations. He continued intelligence-driven tactical operations against the insurgency and improved upon the body of knowledge for his soldiers, creating a jungle manual detailing best practices.[106] In short, he took the balanced framework that Briggs passed him and improved it. The approach applied every available resource and asset at the government's disposal to the campaign. Once the insurgency was brought under control, General Templer's dictator-like power was readily and necessarily abandoned.[107]

Templer's successor, General Sir Geoffrey Bourne, controlled the military side of the counterinsurgency effort while Sir Donald McGillivray served as the High Commissioner.[108] Between 1954 and 1957 a great effort to prepare the Malay government for independence was underway. General Bourne was successful in further destroying the remaining insurgency. As the insurgent ranks continued to thin, the number of surrendered enemy personnel increased. British military assistance was slowly decreased security leadership positions, roles, and responsibilities were transitioning to the Malayans.[109] The thorough British training of the security forces was apparent. The effectiveness, efficiency, and lethality of the security forces did not ebb as the Malays took the reins.[110] The same thing was happening across the country in every government institution. The Malayan government was granted its independence in 1957 and did not have great difficulty defeating the remaining pockets of MCP insurgency that existed in the country.

The twelve-year counterinsurgency struggle in Malaya affords a prime example of the complexity, trial and error, flexibility, and self-evaluation required by a government in order to survive. It took the British the better part of five years, with herculean efforts from Generals Briggs and Templer, to settle on the appropriately balanced strategic and operational approach against the MCP, which ultimately turned the tide of the war to favor the government. During the first two years of the Emergency the focus on heavily weighted, large scale, military kinetic sweep operations were conducted at the detriment of the local people and the integration of civilian agencies. Unity of effort was not achieved and the large scale military operations were decreasingly successful in even gaining contact with the enemy.

General Briggs delivered the first major course correction away from an enemy-centric approach, downgrading the use of large-scale offensive operations in favor of smaller ones and forced military and civilian agencies to work together in the SWECs and DWECs. The security framework that Briggs created, even though he did not get to see it through, would prove to be the foundation of success in Malaya. General Briggs did a great deal to balance the counterinsurgency approach implementing the resettlement program and got a better handle on effective smaller scale kill and capture operations. He fueled an expansion of the security forces and understood the potential of the Home Guard. He implemented both new and improved existing population control programs such as food control, curfews, and registration of the population. Although General Briggs improved unity of effort, his authority to implement his framework and force compliance and focus across the government would prove inadequate. The structure of the decision making process, facilitating decisions by consensus and agreement between the government, police, and military authorities was undesirable and did not result in timely and accurate decisions and their associated implementation.

General Templer was the final ingredient the British and Malayan government needed to achieve an appropriately balanced military-civilian strategy. He was immediately given a huge advantage by being made both the High Commissioner and director of operations in Malaya. He immediately forced the integration of military and civilian counterinsurgency efforts by merging the decision making committees and assigning deputies to answer directly to him. His dictator-esque power was appropriate for the situation. He was able to attain complete unity of effort and expedite the implementation of his decisions. He took General Briggs' sound security framework and both adjusted and added a few additional key components. He understood the counterinsurgency strategy could not be successful without either the passive or active support of the population. He recognized the critical need to retrain the security forces, aggressively grow the Home Guard, and increase the equality and inclusion within the government and security forces of the indigenous ethnic Chinese.

The key intelligence side of the counterinsurgency campaign steadily improved, thanks to the increased presence of Chinese in the army, police, and home guards. As the security forces became more representative of the population, the attitudes of the Chinese population towards the government became more positive. As the reforms in the Malayan security forces took effect, the insurgents had to operate among an increasingly unfriendly population.[111]

Templer relooked the resettled villages and injected money and influence in them to create 'new villages,' drastically improving quality of life, worthy of the Chinese who had been moved there. He expertly utilized psychological operations and set the conditions for surrendered enemy personnel to safely reintegrate into Malayan society. Templer focused his offensive operations against the insurgency to be highly effective, intelligence driven, and precise. He improved his jungle training center and mandated his Officers attend in order to attain the most current operational tactics, techniques, and procedures on jungle warfare against the insurgency. Finally, he set the conditions for transfer of authority to the Malayan government and began to effectively 'Malayanize' the national government and security forces.

After Templer completed the turn-around of the counterinsurgency effort and left Malaya in 1954, the government would not lose the initiative to the insurgency again. One British Army Malayan veteran said one critical political concession predicated success in Malaya.

One word: independence. That's what won it. Suddenly, Chin Peng [leader of the MCP] and all his merry men had the carpet pulled from under them because there they were saying, 'We're going to fight you Brits and drive you out!' And we're saying, 'Yea we're going and we're going to hand it over to Malayans!' There were too many people that had turned against them. All the Malays were against them. Many of the Chinese knew this was going to be a nice and defendable country and wanted a good life. '[We'd] much rather have this lot in charge, than your lot.'[112]

The Malayan Emergency is a good case study to discuss the importance of implementing a balanced Civilian-Military strategy simultaneously utilizing all elements of national power at the government's disposal. In Malaya, the government could not simply focus efforts on the enemy or the population in isolation. They had to construct a hybrid approach that balanced their efforts. A strategy too heavily weighted toward either side, as the Malayan example clearly shows, can prove detrimental to the counterinsurgency effort. "Altogether the Communists' initial success, such as it was, owed as much to the weakness of the Government resources as it did to the strength of its own campaign."[113] The careful application of power, striving for a unified approach across the joint, inter-governmental spectrum offers the best chance for success. A government must analyze each asset it has to apply to the counterinsurgency effort and carefully study the potential second and third order affects the asset can bring to bear against the insurgency. Sometimes the wisest strategic decision involves handing off power to the people who will value it and defend it the most passionately.

Notes

1.   Lucian Pye, *Lessons From The Malayan Struggle Against Communism* (Cambridge, MA: Center for International Studies, Massachusetts Institute of Technology, 1957), 60.

2.   Richard Stubbs, "From Search and Destroy to Hearts and Minds," In *Counterinsurgency in Modern Warfare,* ed. Daniel Marston et al. (Oxford: Osprey Publishing LTD, 2008), 113.

3.   R.W. Komer, "The Malayan Emergency in Retrospect: Organization of a Successful Counterinsurgency Effort" (Research Project, RAND, 1972), 17.

4.   Komer, 17.

5.   J. M. Forster, "A Comparative Study of the Emergencies in Malaya and Kenya," *Operational Research Unit Far East* (1957): Report Number 1/57.

6.   Pye, Lessons From The Malayan Struggle Against Communism, 8.

7.   Komer, "The Malayan Emergency in Retrospect: Organization of a Successful Counterinsurgency Effort," 2-3.

8.   The British government had a difficult time coming to an agreement on how to deal with Malaya at this time. Many within the administration respected and supported the MPAJA after witnessing their success against the Japanese. To several leaders in the administration in the beginning, the Malay Rajas posed a potentially greater threat than the MPAJA to continued British colonial administration in the area.

9.   Frank Kitson, *Bunch of Five* (London: Faber and Faber Limited, 1977), 71.

10.   Pye, Lessons From The Malayan Struggle Against Communism, 9.

11.   Komer, "The Malayan Emergency in Retrospect: Organization of a Successful Counterinsurgency Effort," 5.

12.   Komer.

13.   Stubbs, "From Search and Destroy to Hearts and Minds," 115-121.

14.   Daniel Marston, "Lost and found in the jungle," In *Big Wars and Small Wars*, ed. Hew Strachan (London: Routledge Publishing, 2006), 97-98. The Ferret force were small units that integrated British and Malay soldiers with police. The Ferret force represents British willingness to reform their strategy to better fit the local conditions. Large scale offensive operations were not proving successful. The Ferret force could conduct longer operations in the jungle and better gain contact with insurgents as their signature was small and hard to detect.

15.   The four part Briggs Plan, discussed in detail later in the chapter, would prove effective over time and better balance the strategy. The framework of the Briggs plan would not be changed by General Templer when he took over in 1952, only adapted as necessary to fit the changing conditions.

16. Stubbs, "From Search and Destroy to Hearts and Minds," 118-121.

17. Komer, "The Malayan Emergency in Retrospect: Organization of a Successful Counterinsurgency Effort," 31-33.

18. As part of the Art of War Scholars program, we studied 10 different Counterinsurgency campaigns throughout history including the Philippines, Ireland, Malaya, Algeria, Vietnam, Dhofar, Oman, Rhodesia, Northern Ireland, Iraq, and Afghanistan.

19. Thompson, Defeating Communist Insurgencies, 50.

20. Karl Hack, "The Malayan Emergency as Counter-Insurgency Paradigm," *Journal of Strategic* Studies 32, no. 3 (2009): 385.

21. Pye, Lessons From The Malayan Struggle Against Communism, 7-10.

22. Stubbs "From Search and Destroy to Hearts and Minds," 113 – 115.

23. Stubbs, 8.

24. Pye, Lessons From The Malayan Struggle Against Communism, 15-16.

25. Pye, 18.

26. James Corum, "Training Indigenous Forces in Counterinsurgency: A Tale of Two Insurgencies," (Monograph, Strategic Studies Institute, National War College, 2006), 5.

27. Corum.

28. Komer, "The Malayan Emergency in Retrospect," 25.

29. Stubbs "From Search and Destroy to Hearts and Minds," 115-118.

30. Stubbs, 115.

31. Marston, "Lost and found in the jungle," 97.

32. BI070, Retired General Officer, Interview by Interview by Mark Battjes, Benjamin Boardman, Robert Green, Richard Johnson, Aaron Kaufman, Dustin Mitchell, Nathan Springer, and Thomas Walton, March 30, 2011, United Kingdom.

33. Interview with BI070, March 30, 2011.

34. Hack, "The Malayan Emergency as Counter-Insurgency Paradigm," 386.

35. Stubbs, "From Search and Destroy to Hearts and Minds," 114.

36. Interview with BI070, March 30, 2011

37. Marston, "Lost and found in the jungle," 99-100.

38. Hack, "The Malayan Emergency as Counter-Insurgency Paradigm," 404.

39. Stubbs, "From Search and Destroy to Hearts and Minds," 116.

40. Kitson, Bunch of Five, 75.

41. John Coates, Suppressing Insurgency, An Analysis of the Malayan Emergency 1948-1954 (Boulder, Colorado: Westview Press, 1992), 81-83.

42. Komer, "The Malayan Emergency in Retrospect," 27.

43. Komer, 27-28.

44. Komer, 27.

45. James Arnold, *Jungle of Snakes: A Century of Counterinsurgency Warfare from the Philippines to Iraq* (New York: Bloomsbury Press, 2009), 149.

46. Arnold, 28.

47. Julian Paget, *Counter-Insurgency Operations* (New York: Walker and Company, 1967), 55-58.

48. Paget, 58-59.

49. Paget, 56.

50. Coates, Suppressing Insurgency, 95.

51. Coates, 89.

52. Hack, "The Malayan Emergency as Counter-Insurgency Paradigm," 388.

53. Pye, Lessons From The Malayan Struggle Against Communism, 51.

54. Wade Markel, "Draining the Swamp: The British Strategy of Population Control," *Parameters*, Spring: (2006), 37.

55. K.S. Sandu, "Emergency Resettlement in Malaya," *Journal of Tropical Geography* 18 (1964): 167.

56. Stubbs, "From Search and Destroy to Hearts and Minds," 118-119.

57. Paget, Counter-Insurgency Operations, 58-59.

58. Komer, "The Malayan Emergency in Retrospect," 58.

59. Pye, Lessons From The Malayan Struggle Against Communism, 51-52.

60. Coates, Suppressing Insurgency, 92-93.

61. Coates, 93.

62. Interview with BI070, March 30, 2011

63. Irregular Security Forces are groups that are not members of the traditional government security force systems of Police, Army, etc. The Home Guard in Malaya was specifically created to bolster local security in safe areas in order to allow the government security forces the flexibility and strength to deal with the insurgency.

64. The Home Guard was part of the tiered police system in Malaya. They were the third tier of the system, and lowest level, charged with protecting local villages and key areas denying the insurgency access to their people, food, and

supplies. The Home Guard was an absolutely critical part of the Malay police force as it could secure static areas, in many cases government controlled areas, which allowed additional security forces the flexibility to do other critical tasks to counter the insurgency.

65. Kitson, *Bunch of Five*, 75.

66. Coates, Suppressing Insurgency, 95.

67. Stubbs, "From Search and Destroy to Hearts and Minds," 101-103.

68. Stubbs, 102.

69. Paget, Counter-Insurgency Operations, 61.

70. Komer, "The Malayan Emergency in Retrospect," 27.

71. Coates, Suppressing Insurgency, 85.

72. Hack, "The Malayan Emergency as Counter-Insurgency Paradigm," 388.

73. Hack, 406.

74. Kitson, Bunch of Five, 61.

75. Paget, Counter-Insurgency Operations, 60-61.

76. Leon Comber, *Malaya's Secret Police 1945-60: The Role of Special Branch in the Malayan Emergency* (Pasir Panjang, Singapore: Institute of Southeast Asian Studies 2008),177.

77. COIN Scholars Seminar: January 3rd at Fort Leavenworth. Dr. Marston's Malaya background lecture made a very clear distinction between what the conventional wisdom concerning General Templer's range of power in Malaya vs. reality. Templer did possess near dictator like power when it came to National Policy and the prosecution of the National government's response and efforts against the insurgency; however, he did not control the inter-workings of 8 out of 9 of the Malayan states.

78. COIN Scholars Seminar.

79. COIN Scholars Seminar: January 4-7 at Fort Leavenworth. The history books credit General Templer as a critical component to turning the tide of the Emergency back to favor the government. It became conventional wisdom because of the gains made in Malaya on Templer's watch. Although Templer was a brilliant leader and does deserve the credit he gets, one must remember that Templer implemented, refined, and improved Briggs framework.

80. Komer, "The Malayan Emergency in Retrospect," 30.

81. Komer, 31.

82. Corum, "Training Indigenous Forces in Counterinsurgency: A Tale of Two Insurgencies," 15.

83. Hack, "The Malayan Emergency as Counter-Insurgency Paradigm," 395.

84. Corum, "Training Indigenous Forces in Counterinsurgency: A Tale of Two Insurgencies," 22.

85. Corum, 18.

86. Paget, Counter-Insurgency Operations, 65.

87. Stubbs, "From Search and Destroy to Hearts and Minds," 109.

88. Simon Smith, "General Templer and counter-insurgency in Malaya: hearts and minds, intelligence, and propaganda," *Intelligence and National Security* 16, no. 3 (2001): 65.

89. Smith, 68.

90. Hack, "The Malayan Emergency as Counter-Insurgency Paradigm," 403.

91. Corum, "Training Indigenous Forces in Counterinsurgency: A Tale of Two Insurgencies," 22.

92. COIN Scholars Seminar: January 4-7 at Fort Leavenworth. We debated the importance of the decision to arm the ethnic Chinese in Malaya at length in the seminar class. It was not out of the realm of possible that the arming of the local Chinese could have backfired in a serious way. There was no way to be sure that the armed Chinese the British would empower would not turn on government security forces. It turned out to be the right decision as the issue of the inclusion of the indigenous Malayan Chinese in the government was more important than communist ideology.

93. Corum, "Training Indigenous Forces in Counterinsurgency: A Tale of Two Insurgencies," 23.

94. Paget, Counter-Insurgency Operations, 67.

95. Stubbs, "From Search and Destroy to Hearts and Minds," 110.

96. Stubbs, 110-111.

97. Komer, "The Malayan Emergency in Retrospect," 20-21.

98. Komer.

99. Marston, "Lost and found in the jungle," 98.

100. Marston.

101. Hack, "The Malayan Emergency as Counter-Insurgency Paradigm," 386.

102. Komer, "The Malayan Emergency in Retrospect," 20.

103. Thompson, Defeating Communist Insurgencies, 90.

104. D.J. Wilfurt, "Some Aspects of Anti-Terrorist Operations: Malaya" (22d Special Air Services Regiment, 7th Special Forces Group, Operational Assessment, 1963), 8.

105. Stubbs, "From Search and Destroy to Hearts and Minds," 122.

106. Marston, "Lost and found in the jungle," 103.

107. Komer, "The Malayan Emergency in Retrospect," 31-32.

108. Stubbs, "From Search and Destroy to Hearts and Minds," 126.

109. Komer, "The Malayan Emergency in Retrospect," 21.

110. James Corum, "Training Indigenous Forces in Counterinsurgency: A Tale of Two Insurgencies," 23.

111. Corum.

112. Interview with BI070, March 30, 2011

113. Kitson, *Bunch of Five*, 74.

Chapter 4
Dhofar, Oman
1965 To 1975

An Army can defeat an Army but an Army cannot defeat a people.
If the terrorists come from the people you are not going to defeat
the people and therefore you've got to influence the terrorists in
such a way that they will stop fighting. That is partly by force,
partly by persuasion, and partly by offering them concessions. By
and large of course, the more successful you are militarily, the
more generous you can afford to be in concessions. That is why it
is important that the military side is jolly good.

— BI070, United Kingdom

This chapter will analyze the application of the balanced enemy and
population focused strategy during the Dhofar, Oman counterinsurgency
campaign from 1965 to 1975. While the campaign's scale was smaller
and the socio-political landscape was vastly different than that of
Malaya, many of the same lessons emerged. The analysis will highlight
the Oman government's reform and transfer of authority, which was
critical to achieving a balanced strategy at the national level across the
political, military, social, economic, and psychological lines of effort.
The cooperative execution of counterinsurgency operations in the Dhofar
province by the British Special Air Service (SAS), and the Sultan's Armed
Forces (SAF) and the unity of effort achieved among the SAS, SAF, and
the Sultan produced a highly effective collective strategy against the
insurgency once the British provided more reinforcements to the conflict
in 1970. In Oman, it took regime change from Sultan Said bin Taimur
to his son Sultan Qaboos bin Said on July 23rd, 1970 to set conditions
necessary for creating a sound, balanced, counterinsurgency strategy
capable of defeating the communist insurgency in Dhofar.[1]

The story of the counterinsurgency campaign in Dhofar, Oman is an
important one. Once the conditions were set with the open-minded Sultan
Qaboos in power in 1970, the British, through the Sultan, were able to
create a balanced strategy that simultaneously smashed the communist
insurgency in Dhofar province and produced enough incentive and
opportunity across the lines of effort to convince the majority of locals to
support the government.[2] This campaign further supports the notion that
when fighting an insurgency, a government must take care to foster the right
political climate, open to reform and negotiation. The government must
ferociously target insurgents on the one hand but be willing to reintegrate

insurgents into society the moment they decide to stop fighting. All of this is done while simultaneously partnering with and protecting the local population and providing them tangible standard of living improvements across the security, governance, and development lines of effort.[3]

Oman was never a British colony; however, historically, the British government has had a keen interest in Oman because of its position near waterways critical to transport of key resources and trade commodities. The British government has kept the ruling party of Oman close, establishing lucrative financial arrangements and intermittent military support to maintain the relationship. Prior to the outbreak of the Dhofar insurgency, Great Britain had proved its willingness to come to the Sultan's aid to maintain influence in the country. Between 1955 and 1958, a dispute rose between the Sultan of Oman and a number of Imamates in the country over oil, government policies, and wealth sharing.[4]

The Sultan's Armed Forces (SAF) repelled the uprisings but they did not defeat the groups. They took refuge around the city of Nizwa in northern Oman. The British agreed, in November of 1958, to assist in defeating the insurgency and to help train and equip the SAF to be better prepared for low intensity conflicts in the future. British Special Air Service (SAS) soldiers joined with Sultan's Armed Forces and a British conventional brigade from Kenya to conduct this mission between 1958 and 1959.[5] The British repelled the insurgency and the remaining leadership, the Imamates, fled to the Jebel Akhdar.[6] "It had been victory at the first attempt by a numerically inferior force against an able enemy with geography on his side."[7] Once the British had successfully shifted the momentum of the uprising back to the government and SAF, the SAS withdrew in the same year while detached British officers stayed behind to assist in both training and commanding in the SAF soldiers.[8]

Before delving deeper into this Oman vignette, it is important to draw a distinction between the poor Omani province of Dhofar in the south and the rich Muscat region of Oman in the northeast. Dhofar borders Yemen, referred to at that time as the People's Democratic Republic of Yemen (PDRY) in the West, and Saudi Arabia to the North. The Dhofar province encompasses mostly vast desert, featuring few life-sustaining resources. The largest provincial city is Salalah, bordered by the Arabian Sea to the South and the Jebel Akhdar to the North. The Jebel is a commanding terrain feature that seemingly rises out of the desert north of Salalah, reaching elevations of 10,000 feet in some locations, replete with abundant *wadis*, rocky terrain, and foliage.[9]

The tribes inhabiting Dhofar and the Jebel differ drastically from the northern Omanis. They speak an unwritten language most northern Omanis do not understand, their tribal customs contrast starkly with those of the Omanis, and even their pigmentation is much darker than that of their countrymen.[10] All in all, these regions read as two separate nations. The Dhofaris had been largely left out of the few economic and social programs that existed under Sultan Said. The Dhofaris were a remote tribal people without much reason to support the Sultan and the Oman government. The Dhofar Province with its rugged Jebel Akhdar and Spartan lifestyle is a logical place to base an insurgency.[11] They were the ideal population to sway and co-opt to join an anti-government movement.

After the British SAS left in 1959, the Dhofar province began to experience significant issues in the early 1960s with the rise of the Dhofar Liberation Front (DLF) led by Musselim bin Nuffl.[12] The DLF aimed to separate the province from greater Oman and seize control from Sultan Said bin Taimur, pointing to the enormous disparity between the government's economic and social policies for the wealthy capital city region of Muscat in the North and the much poorer Dhofar region in the south. Because of the lack of opportunity in the Dhofar province, many of the people left the region to work and serve in other countries and were exposed to the outside world. Those that remained behind were easy targets to influence. As the DLF looked to gain outside support, a number of Marxist ideologues offered their assistance. For Musselim bin Nuffl, accepting this assistance would prove a fatal mistake as Ahmad al Ghassani, a Marxist leader supported by both China and Russia, would eventually align himself with enough tribes on the Jebel to take control of the insurgency.[13]

By 1967, the uprising in Dhofar evolved from one aimed at achieving separation from the Sultan's control to a communist-backed, ideological fight for the people of Dhofar by both the insurgency and the Oman government and Sultan.[14] In 1968, the situation took a sharp turn as al Ghassani further radicalized the DLF and clearly articulated the DLFs aim as establishing "scientific socialism"[15] throughout the region. The DLF renamed their group the Popular Front for the Liberation of the Occupied Arab Gulf (PFLOAG). The aim of PFLOAG was to unify all of the Arabian emirate states into one socialist conglomerate.[16] Fighters in PFLOAG had virtual freedom of movement and maneuver on the Jebel in the Dhofar province. The local fighters that made up PFLOAG were referred to as the Adoo, the local word for enemy, by the government forces.[17]

Sultan Said understood the potential danger of PFLOAG and called upon the British to again assist him in quelling a rebellion in his country. The British, who by this time had supported Sultan Said and his exploits for over three decades, understood that this situation was unique and they were not willing to run toward the sound of the guns until a clear political path was illuminated. In many ways, the insurgency had risen because of the Sultan's autocratic policies, rigid beliefs, and unwillingness to reform. Sultan Said followed a strict Islamic interpretation and despised what he was witnessing across the Arab states with the rise of oil revenue.[18] He saw the second order effects of the new founded oil wealth of Westernization and modernization and believed it was severely tarnishing the Islamic way. The Sultan's response to the "devilish secular influence" was to isolate the people in Oman from the outside world. The Sultan banned "trousers, sunglasses, transistor radios, dancing, music, cameras, cigarettes, dolls, and gas cookers"[19] in an attempt to avoid westernization and unwanted influence. To further keep his country devout, the Sultan made life horrible for his people denying them modern medical facilities, schools, and development which led to a massive exodus of intellectuals.[20]

The British knew that if the Sultan was not willing to budge when it came to his beliefs and policies, there would be no way to defeat the insurgency and achieve positive change for the people of Oman.[21] In an interview with a British commander who served in the 22 SAS during the Oman war, he described the British government's recognition that Sultan Said did not possess the political flexibility necessary to achieve success against the insurgency. He stated quite simply that "every war is different but only politics will win and war is about people."[22] He emphasized this point numerous times during our interview stating later that "the military is not going to provide the solution; they are going to provide the pathway down which you've got to go in order to get to the solution. The politicians have got to sort it out. If you are particularly reliant on a military resolution, it ain't going to work."[23] Sultan Said was not willing to even consider a political solution or create programs for the support of the Oman people. Winning a counterinsurgency campaign with Sultan Said was not going to happen. If the British were to intervene and assist against PFLOAG insurgency, the right political conditions had to exist first.

The British government decided it needed to act before it was too late and set political conditions in Oman that could successfully counter the insurgency. PFLOAG was only getting stronger while estimates at the time indicated they were capable of fielding 2,000 fighters with an additional 3,000 militia on the Jebel.[24] Recent conflicts in Malaya and Aden were influential for the British, who were keenly aware that a common strategic mistake was to delay until the counterinsurgency is well organized and established before sufficiently reacting.[25] By 1970, PFLOAG announced that they had complete control over the Dhofar Province and were conducting increased attacks across the country. The final straw came in June of 1970 when the insurgency launched a failed attack on the Sultan of Oman's Armed Forces at their garrison in Iski, in Central Oman.[26] The British knew they had to come to the aid of Oman if they did not want to watch it fall to a communist system. The political situation in Oman would have to be made conducive to both win British political support at home and create a strategy to counter PFLOAG at the national level in Oman.[27]

Sultan Said's son, Qaboos Bin Said was exactly the right leader who the British believed could turn the tide in the war and reform Oman. Said had been allowed Qaboos to leave Oman in pursuit of a Western education in the early 1960s. He graduated from the Royal Military Academy, Sandhurst, and had the opportunity to observe Britain's government structure while in that country. He served a year in Germany alongside his British counterparts and gained an educated Western perspective.[28] Upon return to Oman in 1964, the father quickly surmised that his son had become dangerously westernized and had relaxed his belief system. The Sultan placed Qaboos under house arrest, where he would remain for the next six years.[29]

On July 23rd, 1970 the British assisted Qaboos Bin Said to overthrow his father in a near bloodless coup.[30] The popular impact of Sultan Qaboos taking power in Oman was immediate. For the British, this was the step necessary for the government to further commit to the counterinsurgency effort against PFLOAG in support of the Sultan. Qaboos's rise to power also had an impact on the PFLOAG as well. The new Sultan released his father's chokehold on his citizens by immediately implementing social and economic reforms, retracting racist policies that divided the north and south, and eliminating isolationist policies. Many non-socialist PFLOAG members who had joined the insurgency because of their opposition to the old Sultan found solid reason to stop fighting.[31] Additionally, Qaboos called for a nationwide amnesty and ceasefire to give low to mid-level insurgents a chance to stop fighting.[32] For many of the low level fighters and former DLF members, it was enough to throw down their arms immediately. Hard core socialists in PFLOAG were a tougher sell in that they needed to witness tangible results before making a decision.[33]

Once Sultan Qaboos was in power, the British furthered their commitment to counter the insurgency. They redoubled their support of the SAF, sending more detached and contracted officers to bolster the capability of the current units and raise additional SAF battalions. Lieutenant Colonel Johnny Watts, the commanding officer of 22 Special Air Service (SAS) at the time, had been sent to Salalah, Dhofar Province, in the months preceding Qaboos's rise to power to conduct an assessment of the situation in Oman. His task was to determine how best to increase the SAF's efficiency and which strategy would most effectively counter PFLOAG while bolstering SAS involvement. If this was not daunting enough, he also was to monitor conditions and recommend exactly when to make the move.[34] In an interview between Lieutenant Colonel John McKeown and Colonel Watts, Watts had this to say about the conditions around the city of Salalah and the Dhofar Province in early 1970.

I was horrified. The road was cut and the only resupply was by air or sometimes by sea. . . . There were no Dhofaris in SAF, which was virtually an army of occupation. Everybody on the Jebel was with the enemy, some convinced, some out of boredom, some intimidated: SAF had only a few Jebali guides. . . . There were signs of counter-revolution, with Muslim-Communist arguments. The latter were better armed and organized and ruthless, absorbing some Dhofaris and shooting others. A clash was coming and therefore the Government had a chance of getting some Dhofaris on their side. The idea must be to pick up the Muslim rebellion, but to do this a national aim was needed.[35]

Colonel Watts' assessment of the problems that faced the Sultan's Armed Forces and the way ahead were well received. First, it was very clear to him that the SAF had to get up on top of the Jebel and stay there.[36] The SAF had not had a good experience on the Jebel to date. Every time they went up on the Jebel they had to fight their way out. Colonel Watts envisioned a balanced strategy in which government forces would focus on both partnering, protecting, and controlling the local population, bringing them development, governance, and economy, while smashing the insurgents through intelligence-driven kill or capture operations. None of that could happen until government forces had a secure hold on the Jebel. The current model that was being executed included only offensive operations against the insurgency and was often times void of intelligence. Colonel Watts recommended the SAS be integrated into the Dhofar province as a major player in the campaign. He called it 'Operation Storm' and designed a framework that, in his mind, had the best chance of turning the tide of the war.[37] His campaign plan that would adhere to five basic fronts.

Table 7. Lieutenant Colonel Watts "Five Front" Strategy for Operations in Dhofar, Oman.

1) An Intelligence Cell
2) An Information Cell
3) A medical Officer supported by SAS medics
4) A veterinary Officer
5) The Raising of Dhofari soldiers to fight for the Sultan

Source: Tony Jeapes, *SAS Secret War: Operation Storm in the Middle East* (London: Greenhill Books, 2005), 32-33.

Many Dhofar veterans interviewed had served in both the SAS and the SAF and pointed to Colonel Watts' simple strategy as key and noted the basic concept stuck throughout the war and nested well with the efforts of Sultan Qaboos.[38] It produced the framework for a balanced military approach which advocated both the killing and capturing of the enemy while, at the same time, setting the right conditions to convince the local people to stop fighting and support the government, which now had more to offer.[39] They would use information cell to communicate to both the insurgency and to the locals detailing the good deeds of the government. The medical and veterinarian officer would be used to bring services to the tribal inhabitants on the Jebel for the first time ever. As the primary currency on the *jebel* was livestock, namely cattle, camels, and goats, veterinarian services were sought after.[40] The raising and mentorship of Dhofari soldiers would bolster combat power and facilitate the necessary intelligence required to defeat the insurgency.

This conflict is a prime case study example when evaluating an enemy-centric vs. population-centric strategy. Rather than weighing the strategy to one particular side, Colonel Watts' strategy, and the execution by the SAS and eventually the SAF, created the appropriate equilibrium between two approaches. Even with vastly scarce resources, the scale of which would be unheard of and not even considered for the Contemporary Operating Environment (COE)[41], the men of the SAS utilized every asset or line of effort they possessed, whether bullets, leaflets, medical assistance, or small-scale development and agricultural expertise and applied them evenly to the campaign to win.

One of the first things the SAS did when they got into Dhofar in 1970 was formulate a plan to deny the Adoo freedom of movement on the Jebel. As mentioned earlier, the SAF had a bad experience on the Jebel the months prior, sustaining high casualty rates, and they were mired in a cycle of effectively clearing terrain, but ineffectively holding it. As described in the Malaya chapter, veterans described this as "bait bashing."[42] The SAF would conduct two day missions up onto the Jebel. They would clear villages, search homes, fight, and then head back to their secure base in Salalah, leaving the area vulnerable to re-infiltration.

One SAS veteran commented on the revolving process of bait bashing and the logic behind it. He mentioned that when planning a mission against the insurgency you must understand the second and third order effects and goals of that mission. "If it's [the mission] a short term success that doesn't affect long term aim, it's a failure."[43] Finally, a genuine sense of "*jebelitis*" pervaded the SAF units.[44] *Jebelitis* was a dangerous, almost mystical, fear among the soldiers of the SAF regarding the powerful enemy occupying Jebel. This fear had to be conquered. The only way to do that was to both clear and hold portions of the Jebel.

The SAS did return to Jebel and establish a presence, allowing the SAF to do the same. According to one SAS veteran who played a role in establishing bases on the Jebel between late 1970 and 1972, bases and a permanent presence on the Jebel were early signs that the government was winning and turning the tide of the war.[45] Critical to this effort was the amnesty program internal to SAS and SAF that was in harmony with the Sultan's country-wide amnesty effort. The British were quick to recognize the Adoo vacillated between faithfulness to their religion and loyalty to the hard line communist PFLOAG ideology and belief system that had swept them into the insurgency. The British focused their Psychological Operations (PSYOPS) effort on this fissure with success.[46]

The British and SAF made the insurgency a very simple, black and white amnesty offer that was closely tied to their PSYOPS strategy. The banner phrase for the PSYOPS effort to co-opt and recruit Adoo and other neutral Jebali tribesmen under the PFLOAG banner was "Islam is our Way, Freedom is our Aim."[47] There was no fear of prosecution for Adoo fighters who decided to "cross-over" to the side of the government, even if they had been involved in deadly attacks on government forces in the past.[48] This, coupled with the fact the Adoo could openly practice their religion and gain immediate employment as members of the Firqat, was an attractive offer. The acceptance and implementation of Surrendered Enemy Personnel (SEPs) into the Firqat was hugely significant. In fact, the vast majority of the Firqat were former SEPs. A group of SAF commanders estimated that by the counterinsurgency's conclusion in 1975, 38 tribally affiliated Firqat groups ranging in size from 30–160 members had been formed.[49] The Firqat's end strength numbered well over 1000 fighters when added together and the war would not have been won without them.[50]

The raising of the Firqat required considerable of trial and error. The initial attempt to organize a Firqat group, the 1970 multi-tribal conglomerate "Firqat Salahadin", proved not to be the way ahead.[51] One veteran, who assisted with the formation of a multi-tribal Firqat, indicated the British misunderstood tribal dynamics at the time. Eventually they discovered successful Firqats operated within their own tribal areas and were comprised of singular tribes.[52] Subsequent efforts to raise Firqat groups in singular tribal areas were more successful than previous efforts; however, problems persisted.

Once Firqat groups were raised, British and SAF leaders struggled to control them. Veterans from the SAF commented that, during operation planning, they could count on about a fourth of the Firqat to show up for the mission execution.[53] While the Firqat were a frustrating group to work with, they were critical to counterinsurgency effort. They understood the tribal areas and dynamics, languages, customs, and geography of the Jebel. The British appreciated their unique importance and found ways to work with them. One of the best ways was through the British Army Training Teams (BATT) attached to Firqat groups providing mentorship and enablers including air support and artillery.[54] "The only proven method of enjoying a modicum of control over the Firqat is to have a British Officer or NCO permanently attached. The BATT teams have varied from four men to a dozen or more."[55]

The importance of the amnesty effort resulting in the Firqat program cannot be understated and should raise questions regarding the United States' current amnesty effort in Afghanistan. The amnesty program in Dhofar worked because there was little grey area for a fighter to navigate and consider prior to 'crossing-over' to the government's side. The critical point here is the government forces in Oman recognized there could not be a grey area. If the government wanted to win, they had to allow for reconciliation and integrate the *Jebalis* into the political process.[56] The government could not allow the process to seem threatening in any way. They had to ensure the Adoo believed without question, through both word and action, that when they crossed over there would be no retribution applied against them for past deeds. This required some counterinsurgents to shelve their personal feelings on the matter for the greater good. One SAS veteran described this process as simple math stating, "It is far better to turn one of them [an Adoo] than to kill him. You turn one of them, you've deprived the Adoo of one man and you've gained one. Mathematically that is two. Kill him and so what; he will be replaced by someone else."[57]

At the same time that military operations, coupled with the raising of the Firqat, by SAS and SAF were gaining traction against PLFOAG on the Jebel, Sultan Qaboos launched major economic and development initiatives. Unlike his father, the Sultan had opened the country up to oil export and quickly accelerated the national revenues to 300,000,000 pounds a year. The Sultan took his increased wealth and appropriated over half of it to defense and a large portion to major economic and development projects in Dhofar.[58] Additionally, an economic and development program was an integral part of the strategy at the tactical and operational level within the SAS and SAF aimed at gaining local buy-in within the local communities and the tribes. The SAS and SAF spent considerable periods of time appeasing their Firqat counterparts. Small scale projects were often targeted in loyal tribal areas where Firqats were raised. The Firqat had a voracious appetite for what the SAS and government could bring them.

They [the Firqat] were victims of the cargo-cult. The twentieth century had burst on Dhofar in a matter of months and the Firqat just could not come to terms with all the material possibilities this might bring them; or rather, the SAS teams working with them were hard pushed to meet their demands for blankets, tents, utensils, boots etc. . . . It was common for a young Firqat member to be absent looking after his father's camels for 6 months and to return expecting his back pay.[59]

Once government forces were securely on the Jebel interdicting Adoo freedom of movement, the campaign focus turned to cutting off insurgent supply routes in 1972. In fact, that year would prove a decisive year for the government forces. A couple miles from the border of Yemen, the outpost at Sarfait was established (initially called Simba) to interdict insurgent camel trains coming in to resupply the insurgency.[60] The operation kicked off in April 1972 when the SAF conducted an air assault into Sarfait and immediately began establishing a permanent battalion outpost just a few miles from the border.[61] The bold move to establish Sarfait in such an austere location was the subject of much debate at the time and now.[62] The debate comes because the battalion that occupied Sarfait could do little but sit in their static position and interdict only the convoys that came within visual range. "Sarfait overlooked the routes from Hauf into Dhofar, but the distance from the feature itself to the coast was considerable. Commanding as the position was, there was nothing to prevent enemy camel caravans passing at night through the broken country between the Jebel and the sea."[63]

Many leaders believed Sarfait was a very narrow mission set for an entire battalion and some even wondered if it were a waste of talent.

Others thought that it was an important position for the Sultan to have staked so far to the west. If anything, the position sent a strong signal from the Sultan to PFLOAG and the enemy resupply effort that the Sultan was not willing to cede even the farthest western land he possessed. The audacious move to establish such a position and prove it sustainable, mostly through helicopter resupply, sent an important message to the insurgency. The Sultan and his Army were more powerful than previously imagined and they had the fortitude to win.[64] Sarfait was wildly unpopular with the enemy as the location was close to traditional supply lines. The outpost attracted an enormous amount of enemy activity from the region, including across the border. The soldiers stationed at Sarfait faced heavy enemy contact, including indirect fire from across the border in Yemen. The position at Sarfait took a significant amount of pressure off more strategic areas such as Salalah by giving the insurgency a huge problem to deal with in the west. It forced PFLOAG to refocus many of its assets to deal with the new position.[65]

An additional effort to interdict the insurgents' supply line was executed with Operation Hornbeam that would establish a blocking obstacle between the towns of Manston and Adonib in southwest Dhofar.[66] Although this was a small operation executed by a company, it was important because it laid the groundwork for the larger blocking obstacle effort in the years to come. It was recognized immediately that the position at Sarfait was just the beginning, the anchor point, of a significant effort to cut the enemy off from its supplies coming from Yemen.[67]

In the years to follow, the Hornbeam Line was reinforced with mines and wire while additional lines would be added in the west to interdict the insurgency's ability to resupply.[68] The Hornbeam line was expertly sighted in and was overwatched by a battalion. The strength of this battalion was greatest to the southwest part of Dhofar where the vegetation offered the enemy the best chance to get through under concealment. The SAF forces occupying the line would conduct numerous patrols, nightly ambushes, and complicate enemy resupply efforts. The Hornbeam line would force insurgent camel trains north where they would have to travel further and be forced into more open country where they were easier to identify and engage.[69]

Between 1972 and 1975 the effort to block resupply from Yemen had become a high priority. Added to the defensive position at Sarfait and the obstacle effort was the Diane ring, a series of overwatch positions that interdicted key resupply routes while naturally turning resupply convoys into the Hornbeam line and further north.[70] The Simba and Damavand lines were placed west of the Hornbeam line to provide depth in the obstacle plan and make it increasingly difficult for the Adoo to cross. The Hammer line, named after one of the SAS soldiers serving in Dhofar, was placed just east of the Hornbeam Line.[71] This defensive depth increased the chances of interdicting enemy camel trains significantly. By 1975, the final touches were placed on the obstacle system by connecting the outpost at Sarfait with a mine and wire mixed line all the way to the sea in the south. This ushered the war to a conclusion due to the fact the Adoo could no longer sufficiently supply themselves in their fight against the Sultan and his forces.[72]

On July 19th, 1972 the insurgency, writhing under pressure from the ever-strengthening government forces, planned a bold operation against a small garrison in the town of Mirbat.[73] The Mirbat garrison housed 9 SAS soldiers with an estimated 22 man Firqat in defense.[74] The enemy attacked the garrison with 100 to 200 fighters. The small force of 30 defenders successfully held their position against the overwhelmingly larger force long enough for reinforcements to arrive. A senior Dhofar veteran noted: "One of the 9 was killed, two wounded, but they shared a DSO, a DCM, an MC, 1 MM, and 2 MIDs between them for a remarkable action resulting in 30 enemy dead and over 60 captured. They [the Adoo] never tried a frontal attack this way again."[75] The Adoo's failed attack on the garrison at Mirbat set the Adoo back as they lost a significant percentage of their assembled force. Approximately a fourth of the insurgents had been killed or captured during the attack. The defeat at Mirbat would prove a turning point as fighting in the eastern part of the Jebel waned. The insurgency would not attempt another attack in open terrain against a garrison again.[76]

The Sultan continued his diplomatic efforts as these successful events unfolded. He had joined the Arab League to both continue his efforts to rid the country of his father's isolationist policies and gain outside support. The success of the Sultan against PFLOAG did not go un-noticed by regional partners. The Iranians and the Jordanians, both anti-communist governments, answered the call for help from the Sultan in a measurable way.[77] The Iranians sent their first soldiers, a Special Forces unit, into Oman and began assisting the Sultan with weapons and ammunition in 1972.[78] In December of 1973, the Iranians sent an entire well-equipped brigade to Oman. Most importantly, the Iranians came in with well resourced air and helicopter support that was critical to increasing the effectiveness of the SAF and overall effort against the insurgency.[79] The brigade made a difference by manning static positions both on the Hornbeam line, the midway road and airfield, and closer to Salalah.[80] The Jordanians contributed support as well. They sent intelligence officers and a hefty dose of engineer support that the Sultan desperately needed to bolster his civil support to the Dhofari's.[81]

In 1974, as PFLOAG struggled to sustain its forces and keep pace with the Sultan's efforts, they were compelled to take stock of their efforts. The Sultan's information campaign, amnesty program, development effort in Dhofar, and governance reform was damaging the insurgency as many Adoo decided the fight was no longer worth the cost.

PFLOAG convened its fourth congress in January 1974. A number of problems, including logistical shortages, communications breakdowns, and a high defection rate, were acknowledged. In response to these difficulties, the gradual success of the regime, and the emergence of dissention within its own ranks, the PFLOAG undertook a reappraisal of its strategy. This examination eventually produced a shift of emphasis from the military to the political struggle. . . . The insurgents began to focus almost exclusively on the situation in Oman; therefore the name of the movement was changed . . . to the Popular Front for the Liberation of Oman [PFLO].[82]

The establishment of the first permanent positions on the Jebel in 1973, coupled with the emplaced defensive belt in the west, mostly completed by the end of 1974, tipped the insurgency into defensive mode. [83] The sanctuary area for PFLO had been greatly reduced as SAF and SAS forces. The Sultan's momentum was irreversible. The insurgency failed.

The Sultan took great pains to win over the people of Dhofar and on the Jebel Akhdar using economic and developmental initiatives. As the Sultan opened up his country and pulled his economy out of isolationism. The revenue he had available to bring progress and infrastructure to his people was vastly richer than what the insurgency could bring. PFLO simply could not compete. The Sultan was well aware of the conditions on the Jebel. The tribal people lived an austere life desperately lacking amenities and life support infrastructure. It was easy for the Sultan to bring progress into an area that had nothing. For the people on the Jebel, the most life-altering single resource was water.[84] The water was important to both sustain themselves and to sustain their livestock, which was critical to their nomadic way of life.

Many of the development and economic projects funded by the Sultan on the Jebel targeted Firqat tribal areas to strengthen their support. Areas that begin with nothing laud efforts such as those of the Sultan. One veteran described this process as critically important to the war effort. The Firqat would choose an area for development most central to its tribal lands and the SAF would secure it during the whole process. A Civil Action Team (CAT) would come in and assist in digging a well to make a centralized water point for the tribe.[85] Once the well was built, the CAT would erect a simple infrastructure consisting of a "shop, school, clinic, and a mosque"[86] for the tribal area. The CAT standardized this process across the Jebel to great success. It was a tangible action readily visible to both sides. The action persuaded the Firqat to remain loyal and fueled many other Adoo to stop fighting and join the progress. PFLO could not bring as much to the local people as that government of Oman could. The Sultan also stepped up an already decent effort to develop Salalah and the coastal region of Dhofar. The areas he chose to sink his resources into were areas that were both under the control of and supported by the government.[87]

This is worth considering in light of our own undertaking on the development line of effort in Afghanistan.[88] The Sultan and his forces did want to help the people of Dhofar and bring progress to the area; however, they ensured each developmental initiative was tied to a second and third order effect and the long term aim of the government. In short, nothing was free to the Dhofaris. The Firqat fought with the SAS and in support of the government of Oman. They made the decision not to support PFLO, switched sides, and were doing what they felt was right for their tribesmen. The CATs strategically thought through where they would place their resources on the Jebel. The individual tribes the Firqat represented were the logical choice to gain the most long-term impact for the government. It rewarded the tribes supporting the government and gave them incentives to maintain loyalty to the government. The concept resembled the new village strategy executed in Malaya.[89] The tribes that did not support the government, remained on the fence, or supplied large portions of the Adoo got nothing.

A SAF operation in strength supported by a Firqat secures a position of the Firqat's choice which dominated its tribal area. Military engineers build a track to the position giving road access, followed by an airstrip if possible. A drill is brought down the track followed by a Civil Action Team with shop, school, clinic, and mosque. SAF thins out to a minimum to provide security. Water is pumped to the surface and into distribution systems prepared by military engineers to offer storage points for humans and troughs for animals. Civilians come in from miles around to talk to the Firqat, SAF and Government representatives. They are told that enemy activity in this area will result in the water being cut off. Civilians move out in surrounding areas and tell the enemy not to interfere with what is obviously a good thing [they also provide intelligence]. Enemy, very dependent on the civilians, stops all aggressive action and either goes elsewhere or hides. Tribal area is secure. All SAF are withdrawn.[90]

Psychological Operations (PSYOPS) were repeatedly called critical by nearly every veteran interviewed for this thesis.[91] One veteran interviewed had been involved in PSYOPS for practically the entire war. He made it clear that the PSYOPS effort in Oman was conducted concurrently with every operation they conducted. There was a large leaflet campaign reinforcing the slogans of the government. As mentioned earlier, "Freedom is our Aim. Islam is our Way" was the overall slogan used throughout the conflict. It was chosen to drive home the point that "Islam is prosperous with the Sultan; life is barren with the Communists."[92]

The government had a leaflet campaign and created a radio station in Salalah to provide a counterpoint to a pro-communist station broadcasting from Aden. It even created a mobile movie station, in the days before Salalah had television that could be used in austere locations to broadcast to locals.[93] The PSYOPS director obtained wind up radios to make available to the local population. A lot of thought went into how to help the locals value their radios. After studying the way the Americans had proceeded with a similar radio disseminating effort in Vietnam, the director of PSYOPS in Oman decided to sell them cheaply to increase the sense of ownership by the locals. This was done with the second order effect in mind. If the insurgents destroyed a local's radio, he would be destroying an item for which that local had paid. The idea was that this would anger the local more than if he had been given the item.[94] The most important lesson conveyed by the PSYOPS veteran interviewed dealt with both continuity and aim. He stated "As with any other type of military effort it is vital to keep a clear vision of the strategic and tactical aims at all times. If this is forgotten or neglected it is very easy to expend valuable resources on non-supportive ventures."[95]

The PSYOPS effort in Oman is also worth considering in light of our efforts in the Contemporary Operating environment of Afghanistan. What bound to the fore immediately was that the British were not afraid to confront the thorny issue of religion. They recognized the potential fissure between the communist PFLO ideology and the local customs, religion, and beliefs of the people of Dhofar. They tackled the religious issue head on even though, as with the communists, the British were also a non-Islamic military force. The difference was the British were in support of an Islamic government and recognized the power of the religious differences that existed between the locals and the communists. In Afghanistan, the US has steered as far away from the religious issue as we can.[96]

By late 1975, the insurgency had suffered heavy casualties coupled with an enormous number of defections and they could no longer put up a significant military threat. By December of 1975, government forces controlled all vital areas of Dhofar and reported to the Sultan that is was ready for expanded development.[97] Government forces had increased dramatically in effectiveness and size, the Firqat were supportive and strong in their tribal areas, and economic, development, and governance initiatives were in full swing across the Dhofar province and the country.[98]

The counterinsurgency campaign in the Dhofar province of Oman is informative when compared to the US led war in Afghanistan today. Above all else, it was a struggle for control of the people. Major General (R) Tony Jeapes, who commanded 22 SAS at the beginning of the war makes this point very clear stating "it was first and last a war about people, a war in which both sides concentrated upon winning the support of the civilians of the Jebel Dhofar and which was won in the end by civil development. Military action was merely a means to that end."[99] There were many components to the balanced counterinsurgency strategy in Oman. One veteran described the key components to the victory in his opinion.

Table 8. Winning the War in Dhofar, Oman: The important features.

1) The Sultan's accession and immediate liberal reforms.

2) Sufficient money to expand and equip the forces.

3) Join civil/military control throughout.

4) Airpower.

5) The Iranian contribution.

6) The Government could offer so much more than the enemy.

7) Communism and Islam are incompatible.

8) British Officers.

Source: The Dhofar War (From COIN PRIMARY SOURCES), 19.

The British government was not keen to not further commit themselves until the right political atmosphere was in place to make the reforms necessary to combat PFLO. The British got that reform in Sultan Qaboos, who immediately eased the strict, isolationist policies of his father within weeks of taking power. Sultan Qaboos scrubbed out racist policies across the country, drastically increased economic and development initiatives, increased the funding of the military, and enacted a liberal nationwide amnesty program that gave his enemies a way to re-integrate into Omani society. Most importantly, in spite of the Sultan's drastic reforms in Oman, the tribal system on the *jebel* was reinforced, religion and customs were respected, and they were not expected to change their system. The Sultan had formulated the appropriate strategic level policy that applied the right local solution in Dhofar.

The next step was to form the logical military strategy at the Operational level that was complimentary to the Sultan's efforts and attacked the insurgency from all possible angles. The British military advisory effort, led by the SAS, established a framework created by Lieutenant Colonel Johnny Watts which proved enduring. The framework focused on the local population on the Jebel, injected an economic system in Dhofar, invited insurgents to change sides and immediately employed them in the Firqat, expertly utilized psychological operations, and executed intelligence driven kill / capture operations against the Adoo that significantly reduced the insurgency and made low to mid-level fighters seriously consider 'crossing-over' to the government's side.

Every asset the government forces had at their disposal was utilized with the campaign's long-term aim and goals in mind. It was recognized from the beginning that the military intervention by the British or the expansion of the Sultan's Armed Forces would not achieve victory; rather, they would illuminate the path to a political solution. In the end, with the arrival of Sultan Qaboos, a balanced campaign was established to defeat the insurgency. The military was increasingly effective, the economy fueled a targeted development effort in Dhofar, policies that benefitted northern Oman while ignoring southern Oman were retracted, and the government proved to the local people that their best interests would be served by the government and not by the communists.

While all of these factors were necessary to achieve success against the insurgency in Dhofar, the execution of the government's strategy and the events that unfolded to result in victory were not black and white. Victory against PFLOAG in Dhofar was much closer to the shade of gray. In the military we hesitate mightily to use the word luck; however, there was plenty of it at play for the government forces in this counterinsurgency. As described throughout this paper there was a contentious issue of religion the government exploited to its advantage. Sultan Qaboos himself turned out to be a brilliant, caring leader that his people respected. Had Sultan Qaboos not been able to deliver as the British thought he would, the campaign could have gone the other way. If the Arab League had not accepted Oman into its ranks, the crucial Iranian and Jordanian assistance may have never come. These are just three obvious examples to support the important point that while the victory was sweet for the Sultan and his supporters, the struggle was a close contest to the end.

Nevertheless, the counterinsurgency in Dhofar, Oman will stand as an important and illuminating case study for the governments and militaries that find themselves facing an insurgency. It illustrates a tale in which victory was achieved in an austere environment with few resources and diminutive odds. The Oman veterans did not characterize this campaign as either population-centric or enemy-centric; it was far more complicated than that. One senior veteran stated "the military operations were of secondary importance [to civil action] but of first rate necessity in the first instance."[100] The government achieved a well balanced strategy that aggressively pursued the enemy, partnered with and protected the population, and effectively utilized their resources across the lines of operation to achieve success.

Notes

1.   For the reader that wants to learn more about the counterinsurgency campaign in Dhofar province, Oman, the following literature is recommend. For a great overview of the campaign start Ian Becket's chapter "The British Counterinsurgency Campaign in Dhofar 1965-75," In Daniel Marston and Carter Malkasian's book, *Counterinsurgency in Modern Warfare.* For in depth analysis of the war read General Sir Tony Jeapes book, *SAS Secret War: Operation Storm in the Middle East* and General Sir John Akehurst's book, *We won the War: The Campaign in Oman 1965-1975.*

2.   This campaign represents a rare case-study, along with the campaigns in Greece and Malaya, where a communist insurgency is defeated. The defeat of the Popular Front for the Liberation of the Occupied Arab Gulf, PFLOAG came at an important time for the west as the US was struggling in Vietnam.

3.   BI050, Dhofar Veterans Panel, Interview by Mark Battjes, Benjamin Boardman, Robert Green, Richard Johnson, Aaron Kaufman, Dustin Mitchell, Nathan Springer, and Thomas Walton, March 28, 2011, United Kingdom.

4.   Ian Beckett, "The British Counterinsurgency Campaign in Dhofar 1965-1975," In *Counterinsurgency in Modern Warfare* ed. Daniel Marston et al. (Oxford: Osprey Publishing LTD, 2008), 175-176.

5.   Kitson, *Bunch of Five,* 161-162.

6.   The Jebel Akhdar in the Dhofar Province of Oman is situated in the southern part of the country and would prove to be the perfect insurgent sanctuary area throughout the counterinsurgency. The Jebel, as it is called in short, has peaks that reach as high as 10,000 feet and is surrounded by desert, the city of Salalah, and flat land to the south and rocky no man's land type plains to the north. The Jebel has dense vegetation, steep canyons, and the only way to get to it is to climb or hike up. The force that commands the top of the Jebel holds a distinct advantage over anyone else attempting to gain access.

7.   A. J. Deane-Drummond, "Brilliant but little known British Desert Action: Operations in Oman," *The Times,* April 9, 1959, 14.

8.   Deane-Drummond, 177. For clarity and US understanding the term "detached" when describing British officers who were paid by the British government to serve as commanders in the Sultan's Armed Forces. The British term for this is "seconded" officers. Finally, "contract" officers were those that left the British Army for a period of time and were contracted and paid by the Sultan for service in his Army.

9.   BI050, Dhofar Veterans Panel, March 28, 2011, United Kingdom.

10.   Bryan Ray, *Dangerous Frontiers: Campaigning in Somaliland and Oman* (South Yorkshire, England: Pen and Sword Books Ltd., 2008), 60.

11. Julian Paget, *Counter-Insurgency Operations* (New York: Walker and Company,1967), 24-25.

12. Bard O'Neill, "Revolutionary War in Oman," In *Insurgency in the Modern World* ed. Bard O'Neill et al. (Boulder, CO: Westview Press, 1980), 216-217.

13. O'Neill.

14. D. L. Price, "Oman: Insurgency and Development," *Institute of Conflict Analysis 53* (1975):2.

15. Bard O'Neill, "Revolutionary War in Oman," 217.

16. O'Neill.

17. Bryan Ray, Dangerous Frontiers, 209.

18. John Akehurst, *We Won A War: The Campaign in Oman 1965-1975* (Southhampton, England: Camelot Press Ltd, 1982), 12.

19. Akehurst.

20. Interview with BI050, Dhofar Veterans Panel, March 28, 2011. The Dhofar veterans made it very clear that Sultan Said was falling out of favor with the British government. Because of the Sultan, many of the Oman's top intellectuals left the country if they could. The situation that Sultan Said put country in is analogous to the situation that has faced Afghanistan over the last 30 years. The men with potential and bright futures leave the country if there is no opportunity to be successful. Intelligent, type A leaders are drawn to areas they can achieve success for themselves and their families. In the case of Oman, many left the country and when they wanted to come back in, Sultan Said wouldn't allow it claiming they had most definitely been too westernized and would poison the people's minds with foreign ideas.

21. COIN Scholars Seminar: January 21st at Fort Leavenworth. Dr. Marston's Dhofar Oman background lecture made it very clear that the British were not willing to get involved in the counterinsurgency against PFLOAG because they recognized that in the end, a political solution would have to be reached with the local tribal population in Dhofar to overcome the influence of PFLOAG and their communist ideology on the people. Sultan Said was not willing to budge on his strict Islamic beliefs and was therefore, not willing to negotiate a settlement with the insurgency. The British government recognized that defeating the communist insurgency and gaining and maintaining the support of the local people was not feasible under Sultan Said.

22. BI080, Retired General Officer, Interview by Benjamin Boardman, Robert Green, Nathan Springer, and Thomas Walton, April 3, 2011, United Kingdom.

23. Interview with BI080, April 3, 2011, United Kingdom.

24. Walter Ludwig, "Supporting allies in counterinsurgency: Britain and the Dhofar Rebellion," *Small Wars & Insurgencies* 19, no. 1 (2008): 67.

25. John McCuen, *The Art of Counter-Revolutionary War* (Harrisburg, Pennsylvania: Stackpole Books, 1972), 34-35.

26. Paul Sibley, *A Monk In The SAS: Second Edition* (London: Spiderwize Publishing, 2011), 298.

27. Interview with BI080, April 3, 2011, United Kingdom.

28. BI080, 299.

29. COIN Scholars Seminar: January 21st at Fort Leavenworth. Dr. Marston explained while Qaboos was under house arrest, it was more like virtual house arrest as he was privy to all the perks that the son of the Sultan of Oman would have. Sultan Said honestly thought he was doing the best thing for his son by attempting to isolate him in hopes he would his poisonous western ideas would fade.

30. Ian Beckett, "The British Counterinsurgency Campaign in Dhofar 1965-1975," 179.

31. Bard O'Neill, "Revolutionary War in Oman," 217.

32. Headquarters Dhofar Salalah, "Oman Operations:1970-1975," 1975, 5.

33. Jeapes, *SAS Secret War,* 29-30.

34. Ian Beckett, "The British Counterinsurgency Campaign in Dhofar 1965-1975," 180.

35. John McKeown, "Britain and Oman: The Dhofar War and Its Significance," (PhD diss., University of Cambridge, 1981), 46.

36. Jeapes, *SAS Secret War,* 30-31.

37. Jeapes, 32.

38. In total, 8 SAS veterans and 5 SAF veterans were interviewed who served in the counterinsurgency campaign in Oman between 1965 and 1975.

39. The important point here is that Sultan Qaboos did not try to change the traditional tribal society on the Jebel. He worked to find ways to garner their support without forcing change to their customs and beliefs. PFLOAG did force locals to change their behavior and beliefs when they joined the insurgency on the Jebel. Religion was a one of the main issues. Join the government and continue to pray and remain a devout Muslim. Join the insurgency and give it up. Finally, Qaboos did not take away any of the autonomy of the tribes on the Jebel. He simply wanted them to support the government rather than the communists and searched for ways to prove it was in their interest to do so.

40. Interview with BI050, March 28, 2011, United Kingdom.

41. To say the British government executed this counterinsurgency campaign on the cheap would be a vast understatement. The small teams of SAS that conducted operations in Dhofar and on the Jebel lacked resources that in the modern era of warfare would not be tolerated or considered. These teams went in with a little bit of money, their weapons and basic supplies to sustain themselves but that is all. For a large portion of the conflict, really until the Iranians entered the war at the end of 1973, the SAS had such scarce rotary wing support that casualties had to be carried off the Jebel by donkey. This increased casualty rates significantly. These small SAS teams were successful executing their impossible mission because they were elite soldier leaders that relied on their training and ingenuity to rule the day. They didn't have the luxury, as many of us have the good fortune of utilizing today, of having vast resources to use as leverage within the counterinsurgency campaign.

42. Interview with BI070, March 30, 2011, United Kingdom.

43. Interview with BI070, March 30, 2011, United Kingdom. The lesson on bait bashing is informative for US forces conducting operations in Iraq and Afghanistan. US forces repeated this mistake for years in both countries, planning operations in our forward operating bases (FOBs), executing short-term missions against the insurgency, and then heading back to bases in time for dinner. History shows us this is no way to fight a counterinsurgency and surely does not invite popular support.

44. Jeapes, *SAS Secret War*, 30.

45. Interview with BI070, March 30, 2011, United Kingdom.

46. Headquarters Dhofar Salalah, "Oman Operations:1970-1975," 18.

47. BI060, Dhofar Veterans Panel, Interview by Interview by Mark Battjes, Benjamin Boardman, Robert Green, Richard Johnson, Aaron Kaufman, Dustin Mitchell, Nathan Springer, and Thomas Walton, 2 April 2011, United Kingdom.

48. When Interviewing the Oman Veterans who had served in both the Sultan's Armed Forces and the Special Air Service, they all referred to the process of Amnesty as 'Crossing Over.' The term 'Crossing Over' was a slang word used during the war to describe the process of Surrendered Enemy Personnel (SEPs) joining the side of the Sultan and government.

49. Interview with BI060, 2 April 2011, United Kingdom.

50. John McKeown, "Britain and Oman: The Dhofar War and Its Significance," 56.

51. Middle East Center, "Origins and Formations of the Firqats," Oxford: St. Anthony's College, 1972, Annex A to Section 10, 2.

52. Interview with BI070, March 30, 2011, United Kingdom.

53. Interview with BI060, 2 April 2011, United Kingdom.

54. Beckett, "The British Counterinsurgency Campaign in Dhofar 1965-1975," 180.

55. Headquarters Dhofar Salalah, "SAF Take-Over of Firqat – Dhofar," OPS/D/12 December 28, 1971, 2.

56. COIN Scholars Seminar: January 21st at Fort Leavenworth. Dr. Marston explained this during the seminar as a critical point. To get the insurgents to cross over on the *jebel* there had to be a clearly defined, black and white process to do so. The policy was that no matter what previous operations an individual insurgent had conducted with PFLO, the message was clear (and broadcast) that 100 percent forgiveness and integration would be offered. There was no gray, if an insurgent crossed over his sins were forgiven no matter how many he had killed. Once an insurgent did cross over, he was expected to pass all intelligence he had on the insurgency to the government forces. These crossed over men would be offered employment under the government and would ultimately create the Firqat formations.

57. Interview with BI070, March 30, 2011. The US sticks to its old adage of "We do not negotiate with terrorists," yet near every counterinsurgency campaign that the government "won" did so by reaching political compromise with the insurgency. The US has an amnesty program in Afghanistan; however, it is complicated, biased, and marginally effective. The US amnesty process in Afghanistan is too grey. A fighter who crosses over will be treated differently based on his history. The insurgent who has western blood on his hands or who can be tied to an attack on Western forces will surely consider whether or not he will be prosecuted if he attempted to cross-over to the side of the Afghan government. It is far from the black and white program executed in Oman.

58. John Akehurst, *We Won A War*, 19.

59. WO2 Lane, "Oman Operations: 1970-1975," 27.

60. John Akehurst, *We Won A War*, 300.

61. Headquarters Dhofar Salalah, "The Dhofar War," 1975, 7.

62. It was interesting to see the wide variance of opinion on the merits of the Sarfeit outpost during the interviews with the Oman veterans in both the SAS and SAF. Opinions on Sarfeit ranged from one extreme to the other. Some veterans believed Sarfeit accomplished its mission of interdicting camel resupply lines coming from Yemen. Others believed it was a massive waste of a Battalion as it limited a large number of soldiers to a very narrow mission while critically taxing the sustainment system. Others believed it was an extremely important statement by the Sultan in claiming his territory and sending the message that he was strong enough to sustain such a bold position.

63. Bryan Ray, *Dangerous Frontiers*, 75.

64. BI090, Retired General Officer, Interview by Benjamin Boardman, Robert Green, Nathan Springer, and Thomas Walton, April 4, 2011, United Kingdom.

65. John McKeown, "Britain and Oman: The Dhofar War and Its Significance," 67.

66. Sibley, A Monk In The SAS, 301.

67. Sibley.

68. John Akehurst, *We Won A War,* 60-61.

69. D.L. Price, "Oman: Insurgency and Development," 8.

70. Jeapes, *SAS Secret War,* 189-190.

71. Jeapes, 16.

72. Bryan Ray, *Dangerous Frontiers,* 190-191.

73. John McKeown, "Britain and Oman: The Dhofar War and Its Significance," 72.

74. Headquarters Dhofar Salalah, "The Dhofar War," 1975, 8 (SAS composition at Marbat) and Ian Beckett, "The British Counterinsurgency Campaign in Dhofar 1965-1975, 188. (Firqat strength at Marbat).

75. Headquarters Dhofar Salalah, "The Dhofar War," 8.

76. Beckett, "The British Counterinsurgency Campaign in Dhofar 1965-1975," 188.

77. Ludwig, "Supporting allies in counterinsurgency: Britain and the Dhofar Rebellion," 76.

78. Sibley, *A Monk In The SAS*, 301.

79. John Akehurst, *We Won A War,* 36. The Iranian Brigade was critical in the grand scheme of the campaign as they provided increased air mobility and large formation of soldiers to guard cleared areas and static positions but the British did not respect them as an effective fighting force. The Dhofar veterans described them as dangerously inexperienced and in Akehurst's book, page 84, he details the account of a British company commander coming across the aftermath of an Iranian engagement with the Adoo in which the Iranians had lost 10 soldiers and refers to them as amateurs.

80. John McKeown, "Britain and Oman: The Dhofar War and Its Significance," 81-82.

81. Ludwig, "Supporting allies in counterinsurgency: Britain and the Dhofar Rebellion," 76.

82. O'Neill, "Revolutionary War in Oman," 217-218.

83. Sibley, *A Monk In The SAS*, 301-302.

84. Reid, "Oman Operations:1970-1975," 48.

85. Reid, 49.

86. Reid.

87. O'Neill, "Revolutionary War in Oman," 222.

88. The issue of development in Afghanistan will be covered in the next chapter. In Afghanistan, units have been well resourced with development dollars but, in many cases, have failed to focus their resources to achieve the desired second and third order effects associated with the long term aims of the campaign. Instead, many leaders have utilized development dollars in areas where the local people have made few, if any, sacrifices. Make no mistake, the US military has improved over the years in its focus of development dollars; however, a large portion of what's been spent has failed to achieve much of anything at all. Part of the problem with our effort in Afghanistan is that US leaders may have been resourced too well, which naturally amplified the pressure to spend the resources and make quick progress. The CATs in Oman did not have financial backing anywhere near the levels that the US can access for Afghanistan. The focused development effort during the conflict in Oman may be informative to us today. In the famous words of the late economist Milton Friedman, "There is no such thing as a free lunch." The US military may need to take those words to heart as we continue efforts in Afghanistan utilizing our economic and development might as a key component of our military strategy.

89. Ludwig, "Supporting allies in counterinsurgency: Britain and the Dhofar Rebellion," 92.

90. Akehurst, *We Won A War,* 63-64.

91. The Dhofar veterans pointed to psychological operations as vital to exploiting the narrative of the insurgency and communicating with the local people on the Jebel. It was through the PSYOPS and information campaign that both the government amnesty program and the religious freedom policies were communicated.

92. Dhofar Veteran Manuscript, "Dhofar 1970-1980 a Briefing: A ten year progress from PSYOPS to a Ministry of Information," March 28, 2011, 7.

93. Dhofar Veteran Manuscript, 8-9.

94. Dhofar Veteran Manuscript, 8.

95. Dhofar Veteran Manuscript, 13.

96. For the US military in Afghanistan, religion it is a taboo subject and we feel more harm than good will result from taking it on. This is almost certainly a mistake as the US is allowing millions of uneducated, illiterate Afghans to be persuaded by radical Islamists who preach a version of the Koran that cannot be refuted. Religion in Afghanistan will be discussed in detail in the next chapter.

97. There were still artillery attacks fired from Yemen in the early months of 1976; however, they were largely ineffective.

98. Akehurst, *We Won A War,* 175-176.

99. Jeapes, *SAS Secret War*, 13.

100. Interview with BI080, April 3, 2011, United Kingdom.

Chapter 5
Afghanistan: 2001 to Present

The conditions that really inform your strategy? There is a huge variation at the local level. The challenge is that you are going to have a carrot and a stick and you're going to get variation in the right combination of the two from village to village and within the same village over time. It is a challenge and you have to understand that it's a carrot <u>and</u> a stick and it is not one or the other. It is not an extreme . . . it is the right combination; it is the dynamic application of those incentives and disincentives that will lead to success. One thing General Petraeus would correct you [someone] on in mid-sentence was if they ever made a distinction between kinetics and COIN. He would stop you right there and say, 'Hey, kinetics are part of counterinsurgency, let's not forget that.' But at the end of the day, the strategy has to change to reflect local conditions.

— BA080, Fort Leavenworth, KS

The US war in Afghanistan approaches the completion of year ten at the time of this writing. The conflict has produced, in concert with the counterinsurgency in Iraq, one of our nation's most experienced fighting forces and its longest war, bar none. This chapter analyzes the U.S journey, dating from the first combat operations in October 2001 to the present. The chapter will specifically focus on the "so-called" sequential and differing strategies, Enemy-centric vs. Population-centric approaches, the US has executed over the last ten years and what it took to achieve a balanced strategy that harnesses the best of both in Afghanistan. The chapter will discuss the evolution of the political, military (or security line), social, economic, developmental, and psychological lines of effort, exploring how the U.S has applied them to achieve this critical balance in Afghanistan. Afghanistan presents the US a difficult challenge in the coming years. Here we are, actively pursuing our mission on the cusp of finally hitting the right balanced approach, while, at the same time, popular support for the war declines worldwide.

Afghanistan's history lends context to the current conflict. Afghanistan was born in the eighteenth century when a series of tribes came together to form a dynastic state.[1]

Prior to the Soviet invasion in 1979, a number of tribes ruled the country in succession that belonged to the Durrani dynasty including the Popolzay, Saddozay, and Barakzay tribes through 1978.[2] It is important to understand that, for the most part, those ruling dynasties controlled Afghanistan's foreign policy; however, governance only extended outside the capital city when it was forced, leaving many tribes, sub-tribes, and clans to govern their own regions. Between the country's founding in the 18th century and the Soviet invasion, over 200 years of history, the hearty fabric of Afghan society was formed, which the author witnessed in a fragile state in rural Northeastern Afghanistan in 2008.

The confederation (Ulus) was held together by the common aim of conquering neighboring areas with a view to pillage or exacting tribute. The political and military forms of this period were characteristic of tribal warfare. War was a short-lived affair and decided upon by the council of clan chiefs (a limited *jirga*); the troops that went into battle were selected from the total number of warriors under arms (*lashkar*). The framework was that of traditional society. . . One's allegiance belonged to the restricted group and the tribal code (*pashtunwali*), not to the Pashtun community or to the state . . . 'To exercise Pashtu' (to identify oneself with values) was more important in the context of the tribe than 'to be a Pashtun' (to be identified with an ethnic community or a nation)."[3]

The Soviets entered Afghanistan on December 27th, 1979 and, in the subsequent thirty years; the people of Afghanistan have been at war in one way or the other.[4] The sustained conflict in this country is nothing short of tragic. Afghanistan has endured a failed monarchy, the Soviet invasion, a communist government, the warlord era, the Taliban (*jihadism*), and the Global War on Terror is not over.[5] Its citizens have suffered greatly. For example, by the time the Soviets withdrew from Afghanistan in 1989, 1.3 million citizens had been killed while another third lived as refugees.[6] These figures account for only 10 of the 30 years of conflict!

After the Soviets withdrew in 1989,[7] the Afghan Communist government remained in power for just over two additional years until it was toppled by a conglomerate of ethnically diverse former *mujahedeen* fighters.[8] The years to follow would bring to power a number of tribally aligned warlords in different parts of the country. The Pashtun-backed Taliban came to power in 1996, spreading their strict interpretation of Islam, which barred females from educational opportunities and limited social mobilization. The Taliban set in motion a number of rigid and oppressive laws restricting any concepts perceived as "Western." Osama Bin Laden and Al Qaeda entered the country with permission in 1996. Al Qaeda and the Taliban were mutually supporting as Al Qaeda offered foot soldiers and expertise to support Taliban efforts against the Northern Alliance and in return received sanctuary to train in Afghanistan.[9] They spent the next five years overseeing the training of Al Qaeda members and orchestrating the World Trade Center bombing of September 11th, 2001.[10] Less than one month later, the US launched Operation Enduring Freedom (OEF) in Afghanistan in order to kill or capture Osama Bin Laden, destroy Al Qaeda, and topple the Taliban if they refused to comply with demands to turn over Bin Laden and other Al Qaeda leaders within her borders.[11]

There are a number of theories to characterize the effect of the last 30 years of warfare in Afghanistan. Which theory proves the accurate description depends largely on the area in Afghanistan as each has navigated a different path over time. One theory asserts that new influences began to erode the norms of traditional society. Traditional leaders lost power and influence over some of their men and tribes as new sources of money offered alternatives to customary ways.[12] New economic opportunities, such as receiving money for fighting, opened new social mobility platforms outside of the traditional tribal structure.[13]

After 30 years of conflict, an economy has developed in which money is exchanged for fighting. Violence has created the most viable path to social and economic mobility and political influence. Those who prove skilled and demonstrate leadership qualities can advance in the ranks, increase their local power, and grow wealthy. Many insurgent leaders are from traditionally poor families who would otherwise have remained outside the local governing structures.[14]

Another theory asserts the relevance of the traditional leaders' loss of power over the last 30 years is overblown and religion lies as the true motivation of the insurgency. "Westerners have not come to the realization that this insurgency is an Islamic jihad. The insurgency's root cause is not lack of economic opportunity, but the desire to establish an Islamic Emirate of Afghanistan under *Sharia* law."[15] The author goes on to assert that the influence of the mullah, not the traditional khans and elders, is at the heart of the insurgency.[16] The reality is that all of these theories are partially correct, depending on the local area, and add to the complexity of the geo-political landscape of Afghanistan. As David Galula would say, to be successful in this type of conflict, "build (or rebuild) a political machine from the population upward."[17]

A couple months after the US entered Afghanistan in 2001, the Bonn conference was conducted to reestablish an interim government authority and constitution, create baseline laws and procedures, garner international support for the new government, and secure the financial assistance necessary from the international community to move forward.[18] The Bonn conference was well received by the international community and gave Afghanistan a starting point from which to expand. The international community, led by the US in late 2001, worked tirelessly to establish the government in Kabul and assist in creating the institutions necessary for it to run efficiently as quickly as possible.

From the beginning, the central government has been fraught with issues ranging from illegitimacy to corruption. Its success is seen today as critical to US policy.[19] Initial focus and mentorship at the central government level came at the expense of appropriate focus at the provincial and district government levels. The key issue was connecting those mid-level governance systems with the well-established tribal governance at the local village level. Efforts are now being made to improve sub-central governance. "There has been a US shift, predating the Obama Administration, toward promoting local governance. Some argue that, in addition to offering the advantage of bypassing an often corrupt central government, doing so is more compatible with Afghan traditions of local autonomy."[20]

The changes in the strategy and focus of military operations in Afghanistan over the last 10 years can be illustrated by a pendulum. From the start of the war until General McChrystal's 2009 strategy reassessment, the operational strategy weighted heavily on the security line of effort that highlighted kill or capture operations against the enemy while the other lines of effort, political, social, economic, developmental, and psychological, were deployed in support. The singular focus on kill or capture operations was in no way the only strategy being implemented by coalition units across Afghanistan. There were plenty of success stories utilizing a wide variety of different approaches to achieve success and momentum in individual AOs.[21]

As Afghanistan became a secondary priority due to the Iraqi war from 2003 to 2009, both troop levels and total funding were insufficient to do much else effectively. Troop levels have slowly increased in Afghanistan since the war's early days, beginning at 10,000 in 2002 and ending up right at 69,000 by December of 2009.[22] By now, May 2011, well over 90,000 US troops serve in Afghanistan. This raises another complicating issue that has hindered the States' ability to achieve a unified strategy. With such small numbers of soldiers in Afghanistan, the level of autonomy individual commanders had on the ground, from the company to the brigade level, was as vast as the Areas of Operation (AO) they controlled. For example, there was only one brigade combat team in RC-East in 2005. That number doubled by 2008 and as of May 2011, there are four maneuver brigades in the AO.[23]

While each unit certainly learned lessons at the local level, some commanders failed to adequately adapt to their environments. Some areas achieved significant progress while others slipped deeper into conflict. Commanders who understood their environments experienced this autonomy as a great asset; however, it was a dangerous concession to those who did not or would not deviate from their original strategic plans and assumptions. General Sir Frank Kitson makes it clear that good officers develop characteristics that allow them to adapt to their unique areas of operation.[24]

Those [officers] who are not capable of developing these characteristics are inclined to retreat into their military shells and try not to notice what is going on. They adopt the 'fit soldier with a rifle' theory, and long for the day when they can get back to 'proper soldiering' by which they mean preparing for the next-or last- war, as opposed to fighting in the current one. . .Considerable progress in subversion and insurgency could be achieved by careful briefing of those commanding units.[25]

Many commanders rigidly oriented their units to killing and capturing the enemy each day even though their AOs were conducive to partnering with and protecting the population while utilizing political, economic, development, and psychological initiatives to enhance their efforts. In order to combat this, ISAF issued a series of tactical directives to assist commanders to better understand the operating environment and the potential skills necessary to be successful.[26] The problem grows exponentially when you add the unique national caveats of each ISAF contributing country.[27] It is similar to bait bashing, as referred to in both the Malaya and Oman chapters and experienced by the author in Operation Iraqi Freedom II. Highly skilled units would coordinate complex mission after mission to disembark from their compounds, kill or capture the enemy and clear the terrain but they relinquished all ground gained at the day's end, returning to the Forward Operating Base (FOB) in time for dinner. The cycle caused units to constantly clear the same areas.[28]

The opposite was also true. Other commanders bought into the population-centric strategy wholesale and misdiagnosed the root causes for conflict in their areas. It was easy to be blinded as senior leaders and practitioners. Some were fresh off successful surge experience in Iraq while others learning the same lessons in Afghanistan began largely saying the same thing, the silver-bullet in Afghanistan lies with winning the support of the population.

The future is not one of major battles and engagements fought by armies on battlefields devoid of population; instead, the course of conflict will be decided by forces operating among the people of the world. Here, the margin of victory will be measured in far different terms than the wars of our past. The allegiance, trust, and confidence of the populations will be the final arbiters of success.[29]

They believed so fervently in the new doctrine, partnering with and protecting the people while leveraging the political, economic, development, and psychological lines of effort, that they were blinded to the objective truth. The insurgency had grown too powerful in their areas of operation and required clearing before any hope of progress could be achieved. A brigade commander made clear that the enemy has to be dealt with effectively before the other lines of operation can have the impact desired. "Find the enemy, fix the enemy, kill the enemy, and then expand out and protect the people."[30] There is no silver-bullet approach. An ISAF advisor stated, "Doctrine is great but it is not dogmatic and must be interpreted based on local conditions."[31] Both the population-centric and enemy-centric approaches can prompt a leader, sometimes unwittingly, to reveal his affinity for one over the other. It follows that he would prefer to prove his approach superior. The debate over the superior tactical approach has impeded some units' abilities to effectively analyze situations on the ground in real time. It has created a mythical ideal scenario that could hinder creative thinking and bias the people whose lives depend upon objectivity. There is no substitute for objective, flexible leadership and strategy planning and openness to all lines of effort.[32]

To further complicate matters, each AO exists within a fundamentally unique and nuanced environment at the local level, which complicates a senior commander's ability to evaluate whether a subordinate commander is pursuing an appropriate local strategy. "Operations in Afghanistan from 2001 to 2009 have been marked by a series of disjointed efforts to learn how to conduct counterinsurgency in Afghanistan."[33] Counterinsurgency guidance continued to evolve. General McKiernan, commander of ISAF from 2008 to 2009, published COIN directives on March 18, 2009 that looks similar to the guidance today. "Our operational imperative is to protect the population while extending the legitimacy and effectiveness of the GIRoA and decreasing the effectiveness of insurgent elements."[34] One commander interviewed was tasked to implement McKiernan's guidelines across the country in 2008. "I traveled around the country to help implement his guidance; I was his COIN team. I found that units were just not implementing the guidance, they were doing counter-terror."[35] The charge to shift the strategy was in place under McKiernan but executing the protocol was a different story. It is vital to convey that many leaders from that period accepted the COIN guidance, understood their AOs intimately and pursued intuitive, highly successful strategies that positively contributed to the war effort.[36]

Shortly after General Stanley McChrystal took over as the commander for the International Security Assistance Force (ISAF) he assembled a strategic assessment team to review the war in Afghanistan.[37] On August 30, 2009, General McChrystal released his Afghanistan strategy assessment. It advanced COIN concepts created under McKiernan, challenged conventional wisdom, and set a new tone for our military strategy.

ISAF is a conventional force that is poorly configured for COIN, inexperienced in local languages and culture, and struggling with challenges inherent to coalition warfare. These intrinsic disadvantages are exacerbated by our current operational culture and how we operate. Preoccupied with protection of our own forces, we have operated in a manner that distances us–physically and psychologically–from the people we seek to protect. In addition, we run the risk of strategic defeat by pursuing tactical wins that cause civilian casualties or unnecessary collateral damage. The insurgents cannot defeat us militarily, but we can defeat ourselves.[38]

General McChrystal's 2009 strategy reassessment determined the operational strategy focused too heavily on kill or capture operations and needed more balance to harness the potential benefit from all available assets and lines of effort. The mission statement of ISAF became population-centric in 2009.[39] "ISAF, in partnership with GIRoA, conducts population-centric counterinsurgency operations, enables an expanded and effective ANSF and supports improved governance and development in order to protect the Afghan people and provide a secure environment for sustainable stability."[40] Over the next year, General McChrystal and his ISAF team produced tactical directives encouraging commanders to focus on the Afghan population and communities rather than just the enemy.[41]

Progress and reform occurred on General McChrystal's watch, in part, because the ISAF mission statement directed soldiers to conduct population-centric counterinsurgency operations but in some areas the pendulum swung too far from the balanced approach that was envisioned.[42] Some units interpreted the ISAF tactical directive guidance in stark black and white. Junior commanders often took statements such as "the use of air-to-ground munitions and indirect fires against residential compounds is only authorized under very limited and prescribed conditions"[43] out of context. In the name of complying with the commander's intent, some units centralized their indirect fire and close air support (CAS) procedures and, in turn, constrained their junior formations in contact. Although ISAF intended to limit civilian casualties by decreasing the use of indirect fire and CAS, the new mission statement was never intended to constrain commanders or endanger soldiers in contact.[44] Clarifying remarks on the same page of the directive make this evident. "I cannot prescribe the appropriate use of force for every condition that a complex battlefield will produce. . . This directive does not prevent commanders from protecting the lives of their men as a matter of self defense when it is determined that no other options are available to effectively counter the threat."[45] Nevertheless, the rules of engagement would be reviewed regarding the employment of CAS and indirect fire when General Petraeus assumed command of ISAF months later.[46]

One vital area that became a higher priority was Afghanistan's National Security Forces (ANSF) and ISAF's effort to develop and expand them. By October 2011, the goal is to have a 305,000 man ANSF.[47] In short, General McChrystal and his team expanded the ANSF effort while redefining the procedure for partnering our forces with Afghanistan's local military forces. "The requirement to expand the ANSF (both ANA and ANP) rapidly to address the challenges of the insurgency will require ISAF to provide enhanced partnering, mentoring, and enabling capabilities until parallel capabilities are developed within the ANSF."[48] The rapid expansion of the ANSF has caused problems. Partnering and mentorship of the ANA was more natural for the military and as a result, their progression has been faster than the ANP.[49] "The United States and its partners still have not centered on a clearly effective police training strategy."[50] ISAF has amplified efforts with the police in 2010 asserting that a well trained and capable police force is at least as critical as an ANA force.[51]

President Obama followed General McChrystal's strategy assessment by delivering a speech in December of 2009 that officially cast the Afghanistan war as the primary focus of the United States. He committed an additional 30,000 soldiers to shift the war's momentum and he invested resources to further solidify our partnership and cooperation with Pakistan. President Obama clearly accompanied his calls for victory with ample resources to deliver one. Afghanistan was now the priority.

I am convinced that our security is at stake in Afghanistan and Pakistan. This is the epicenter of violent extremism practiced by al Qaeda. It is from here that we were attacked on 9/11, and it is from here that new attacks are being plotted as I speak. This is no idle danger; no hypothetical threat. In the last few months alone, we have apprehended extremists within our borders that were sent here from the border region of Afghanistan and

Pakistan to commit new acts of terror. And this danger will only grow if the region slides backwards, and al Qaeda can operate with impunity. We must keep the pressure on al Qaeda, and to do that, we must increase the stability and capacity of our partners in the region.[52]

When General Petraeus took over as the commander of ISAF in July of 2010, the counterinsurgency strategy did not change but it was refined. The tactical guidance and rules of engagement were reviewed regarding CAS and indirect fires procedures and General Petraeus opted not to change the standing directive the General McChrystal had ordered. He did clarify the ROE and ensured subordinate commanders understood when it was appropriate to use fires and that they did not have the authority to apply additional procedures to the fires process. "Subordinate commanders are not authorized to further restrict this guidance without my approval."[53] Additionally, the term population-centric was removed from the mission statement and replaced with a less black and white term to direct soldiers' actions in Afghanistan: conducts operations.

In support of the Government of the Islamic Republic of Afghanistan, ISAF conducts operations in Afghanistan to reduce the capability and will of the insurgency, support the growth in capacity and capability of the Afghan National Security Forces (ANSF), and facilitate improvements in governance and socio-economic development in order to provide a secure environment for sustainable stability that is observable to the population.[54]

The new mission statement swung the pendulum back toward the center, resulting in the most balanced approach in Afghanistan to date.

The US has struggled to get a handle on the political and governance lines of effort since the genesis of our efforts in Afghanistan. As mentioned at this chapter's beginning, federal governance has never really extended beyond the confines of the capital city, Kabul. Historically, the King or Amir controlled foreign policy and dealt with the ethnic tribes surrounding Kabul when necessary.[55] Autonomous, self-reliant tribal groupings comprise over 80 percent of rural Afghanistan and always have.[56] While the Afghan government historically has avoided conflict and even contact with the tribes, the same phenomenon exists in reverse. In short, there are many self-contained, independent tribal and local groupings within the confines of Afghanistan's border, all with their own identities, traditions, goals and values. These tribes and local groups are only tangentially associated with the central government and their politics are purely local.[57]

To complicate matters, the US led coalition attempted to install a Western style Jeffersonian democracy at Afghanistan's central governance level in 2001, which has been an ordeal to integrate. While this western governance construct was welcomed as the way ahead by interventionist powers such as the US and other members of the Western international community, it was foreign to Afghans. "Our failure to reinstate King Zahir Shah to his throne is an example of our lack of understanding of the Afghan condition. A true parliamentary democracy with the king as the head of state [as had been the tradition in the past] could have provided solutions for problems coalition forces faced [with Afghan governance]."[58] The US has doggedly pursued this endeavor at the central level, committing extraordinary resources and time in an attempt to make it work. "Most of the coalition's efforts have centered on initiatives such as the creation of the heavily centralized Afghan government ministries."[59] This misguided effort belies the fact that, for much of the conflict, the US and its allies have lacked a fundamental understanding of how traditional Afghan society functions and the relationship, or lack of one, between the rural tribes and the government.[60]

As a troop commander in Northeast Afghanistan for 15 months in 2007 and 2008, the author was stunned to discover traditional governance at the tribal and village level not only functioning, but thriving. It did not take long to conclude that local tribal politics afforded Afghan young men a significantly more democratic system than the Afghan top-down, ministry-heavy, central, provincial, and district government forms did. In the rural Pashtun and Nuristani areas the author commanded, local *Jirgas* occurred weekly or bi-weekly, depending upon the area, with the expectation that every male attend.[61] Attending a *Jirga* was a revered right and inextricably bound to each tribe's heritage. The striking similarities between *Jirgas* and Greek-style democracy were surprising. Each man in the *Jirga* had the right to voice his opinion and the author found it fascinating, and sometimes frustrating, that decisions weren't made unless there was 100 percent, or very close to 100 percent, consensus within the group. As a young Captain charged with accomplishing tasks quickly and efficiently, the author struggled to adjust to this more methodical governance style. The author learned to accept the *Jirgas* would not take one step forward unless overwhelming evidence compelled them all to agree it was in their best interests to do so. Tribal governance did not need fixing in the area.[62]

Herein lay the real challenge associated with Afghan governance. This highly competent traditional tribal democratic system had operated adequately for centuries when along came the Bonn conference and its newly minted, western-influenced central government. This new central government model featured district, provincial and central governance levels, reminiscent of the US local, state and national government levels.[63] The monolithic new government system needed credibility but how could it assert authoritative power within this enduring political landscape of tribal governance? To further complicate matters, the central government offered (and continues to offer) very limited assistance to tribal and local governments and, throughout history, whether king or Amir, this pattern has persisted. The city dwellers in and around Kabul have far more access to services and hard evidence that a central government can benefit them.[64]

The tribal populations of Afghanistan have little incentive to cooperate with the central government because it is absent from their lives and, as we've learned, the *Jirgas* do not ratify change without justification and consensus. ISAF unintentionally fueled the perception of an incapable central government by delivering services in any way they could to the local areas, with little central government involvement. "The degree to which Afghans feel a part of what is at stake in their country and to what has been achieved so far is unclear. . . Finding ways to empower Afghans in Afghanistan emphasizes the importance of an integrated approach and one that builds needed capacity on multiple levels."[65] The tribal populations need to witness the central government delivering goods and services, not the ISAF, if they are ever to believe in it.

Since 2001, presented with an Afghan central government whose presence at the local level has often been either absent, incompetent, or corrupt, the international community has turned increasingly toward nongovernmental organizations for the delivery of services. Yet this approach rarely strengthens the perceived legitimacy of the government in the very communities whose loyalty to the government is being contested.[66]

As part of General McChrystal's Afghan strategy assessment, he articulated what so many of us had come to believe on the ground: the central government must find a way to respectfully link up with the well-established tribal and local governance systems to become relevant. "We must facilitate the development of governance capacity that serves the interests of the people. Until the government is seen as less hostile to those interests, it will never gain trust and respect."[67] McChrystal's report highlights the governance leaders' vastly varying degrees of competency at the provincial and district levels. He asserts the ISAF must prioritize efforts to remediate and fortify governance efforts at these levels.[68] Although the US and ISAF have expanded efforts to increase government transparency, efficiency, and effectiveness at the district and provincial stations, a number of concerns remain. Nevertheless, the important first step of connecting the central, provincial and district government system with the local people of Afghanistan has been acknowledged.[69]

Tremendous issues still beg resolution. For instance, under the central/provincial/district system, President Karsai currently appoints all provincial governors, even if they do not hail from the provinces they govern. Karsai grants the provincial governor's authority to appoint district governors and many of these appointees also have no connection to the districts they are tasked to oversee. The system is patrimonial. Financial and business considerations often factor more heavily into these governor decisions than questions relating to leadership or honest governance for the people.[70]

The Afghan people are very well aware of the graft and corruption. None of them [the provincial and district governors elected] live where they are elected and they do not spend any time there. Why is that? Because now that they have been elected, they can make some money by going to Kabul, Jalalabad, Kandahar, or wherever there is money to be had. The people know that so they don't put a lot of stock into government.[71]

These governors were neither respected nor recognized by the local men, villages, and *Jirgas*. The locals viewed their governors as mere obstacles who had to be dealt with daily.

One senior commander who has completed multiple Afghan tours of duty offered his view on an important step we must take immediately if we hope to gain the buy-in of local people.

We need to reinforce existing customs and existing mores that they have like the tribal *shura*. The purple finger thing is just not going to work in Afghanistan, it just isn't. It's nice, it's symbolic, just like that picture of Karsai, but it means nothing. What means something is if the *shura* elders are the ones who elect their District governor. You do that and all the sudden they have invested in that District governor. He is beholden to them, the people of that district that he represents, and especially the elders. Then he argues with the Provincial governor for what they need. Wouldn't it be great if you had all the elders in a Province elect the Provincial governor they want or the District governors elect the Provincial governor they think will be most effective?[72]

As a battalion commander explained, leaders at the tactical level must ensure the traditional governance construct at the local and village levels functions well and then find a way to connect it with the district government.[73] There is a difference between governance and government and tactical level leaders are largely concerned that governance functions fluidly before concerning ourselves with government.[74] Connecting the two is the important next step and one ISAF and the international community must achieve.

Harnessing the development line of effort in Afghanistan has also been a challenge during the conflict. At every level, focusing our development and economic targets to achieve positive second and third order affect has been hit or miss. As the counterinsurgency effort has progressed over the years, significantly greater monetary assets are available to commanders.

US government funding for assistance has come through three main agencies – The Department of Defense (DOD), the US Agency for International Development (USAID), and the State Department. Military and security assistance since 2001 represents more than half of US funding for Afghanistan and has been provided through DOD, mainly through the Afghan Security Forces Fund, the Commander's Emergency Response Program (CERP), and other funds appropriated for counternarcotics and other programs.[75]

As the availability of development dollars multiplied for commanders in Afghanistan, so did the pressure to use them. Success and failure in the application of development assets is unique to the local area and the way each commander individually utilizes and applies his development dollars.

US government funding for development and aid has been the subject of much debate during the course of the war. The success stories highlighting how development dollars facilitate troop-population relationships and further a unit's strategy. The 1st Squadron, 91st Cavalry, 173rd Airborne Brigade lived a few of those stories. Development dollars enabled the unit to oversee the successful construction of hydro-electric plants, pipe schemes, bridges and factories, putting locals to work and truly improving their living conditions. The use of Development as a catalyst for the start of a relationship with one remote village community was most telling.[76]

In the town of Saw, Naray District, Konar Province in Afghanistan, just 13 kilometers from the FOB, villagers had wanted nothing to do with the unit when it first arrived in summer 2007. The village had been a coalition ally up until the previous year, when an unsuccessful nighttime search operation brought soldiers in pursuit of a high-value target straight into villagers' homes, where many women were mortified to be seen uncovered. The village men considered themselves disgraced. The village elected to terminate relations with the coalition over the incident.[77] The newly arrived 1-91 Cavalry began the delicate process of mending the rift. 1-91 leaned heavily on the partnered Afghan Army battalion and engaged in hours of earnest informal meetings with community leaders who had heard the new unit was operating differently. Slowly, the 1-91 began to make progress re-establishing the trust and respect lost. First, 1-91 Cavalry tasked the

Afghan Army with delivering some very basic Humanitarian Assistance (HA) including school supplies to the village. Next, the unit empowered village leaders to start small projects using development dollars. The village began to believe the unit and, by extension, the central government was trustworthy and had something to offer. Over the next many months with the Afghan Army in the lead, the trust was re-earned and the village became a close ally.[78]

There are just as many stories of development dollar failure and those truly happened as well. As with most experiences, the leaders who dismiss development dollars as a waste of money and time are the same ones who have negative experiences applying the assets in their areas. The issue becomes black and white, as if there is a solid answer one way or the other as to whether development efforts are worthwhile. This is one issue in which the debate sounds the same whether the topic is Afghanistan or Iraq. The conversation begins with statements such as: "Nonlethal enthusiasts of COIN orthodoxy claim that combat operations, even if successful, bring only a temporary dip in violence. They contend that projects and services provide more long-term benefits."[79] The application and use of development dollars does not equal the panacea for success in Afghanistan. There is no single component that does. If there were one, the war in Afghanistan would have ended long ago. Development efforts do represent a key critical enabler that is germane to a balanced strategy as proven in the case studies of Mayala and Dhofar in the two previous chapters.

The 1st Squadron, 91st Cavalry, mentioned above, experienced both successes and failures following development dollar projects in Afghanistan. The critically important lesson learned was that a unit does not have to spend money just because it can. Each project must have a long term aim and the second and third order affects must be fleshed out and scrutinized to ensure the effort is worthwhile and does not feature tangentially associated consequences that the unit failed to anticipate. There were plenty of development initiatives the unit got burned on in the beginning of the last tour to Afghanistan; however, once leaders began to understand the potential of each development dollar, they learned to apply the funds more effectively.[80]

In the end, the application of development resources using initiatives such as CERP, ASP, or work for food programs are important components and enablers to the strategy in Afghanistan. The US cannot allow itself to enter circular debates that have no logical right or wrong answers. Development dollars, assets, and initiatives represent enablers our enemies do not possess. The US must wisely employ these assets to potentially fuel its efforts while hobbling theirs. Whether a commander can effectively use development in his AO is often dictated by the local situation and enemy threat, but sometimes it is limited only by his capacity to comprehend the local dynamics of his AO. Regardless, the last thing the US can afford to do is remove this asset from the table.

The information or psychological line of effort has improved considerably since the beginning of the war in Afghanistan; however, outstanding issues remain. One of the most resounding improvements since the beginning of the war has been the military's simple acknowledgment of the significance of information operations. Resourcing these efforts has been dramatically improved across the country. Even though a shortage of Psychological Operations Officers (PSYOPS) is still a problem, the US military has procured a number of items to facilitate information operations at the unit level.[81]

Recognizing the desperate need to counter insurgent propaganda at the tribal level, the United States military started the radio in a box program in 2006.[82] This program brought an asset normally utilized at higher echelons down to the battalion and even company levels. The program provides the equipment and funding necessary to hire Afghan personnel to run a radio station that broadcasts command information, interlaced with traditional Afghan music and news. Wind-up radios are provided to locals through Humanitarian Assistance channels. The technique of handing out radios to the local population was debated by one Oman veteran. He stated "radios were sold at cost in Dhofar province to increase the sense of ownership by the locals that purchased them. That way, when the insurgents came through and destroyed a local's property, it increased their outrage as they had not been given the radio, rather, they had bought it themselves."[83] This is an important consideration the US missed in the application of its information operations campaign in Afghanistan.[84] Nevertheless, the radio in a box program enables commanders at the tactical level to quickly broadcast important information to locals in the area, confirm or deny rumors, and quickly counter insurgent propaganda.[85]

Important lessons regarding Information Operations (IO) and PSYOPS can be drawn from the previous case studies in this thesis to further improve our efforts in Afghanistan. The US has severely limited itself with regard to IO when it comes to issue of religion. "With overwhelming firepower, Western armies rarely lose in combat to Taliban fighters in Afghanistan but in the communications battle, the militants appear to hold the edge."[86] They hold the edge because we have treated religion in Afghanistan as a subject we must avoid. This gives the insurgency a huge advantage. As there is a very low literacy rate in Afghanistan, the Koran is taught and interpreted to most by religious leaders in their community. If those religious leaders are sympathetic to or coerced by the insurgency, then the religious education of the local people skews against the coalition or Afghan government.[87]

In Oman, the British did not avoid religious differences they perceived between themselves, SAF, and the Firqat. They used religion to drive a wedge between the communist backed insurgency and the Islamic government of Oman with a lot of Omani support. In Afghanistan, the potential to clear the same hurdle exists. The insurgency in Afghanistan is obviously not communist; however, it purports a strict and rigid Islamic interpretation not shared by Afghanistan's government or the majority of its people.[88] ISAF, in close consultation with the Afghan government, does not have to cede the religion issue to the insurgency. The increase in IO funding in ISAF for resources such as Afghan run radio stations and newspapers have huge potential to be leveraged further.[89]

ISAF can tackle the religion issue by empowering the Afghan government and our Afghan partners to better utilize resources to launch a religious education program across the country. The Afghan government, with the support of ISAF resources, has the opportunity to turn the corner on this critical issue and combat radical religious interpretation and teachings. ISAF can help supply the resources and assets to do so; however, it must be an Afghan run program to solve a critical Afghan issue.

As leaders gained experience in Afghanistan, each came back with vastly different ideas of what worked and what did not, based on their individual AOs. One of the debates that emerged is whether the military should focus on killing or capturing the enemy or partnering with and protecting the population from the enemy. This is commonly referred to as enemy-centric or population-centric COIN. Open debate within a military is constructive; however, the debate can quickly turn inflexible when that debate is based on personal, emotional experiences and, sometimes, troop losses. Value diminishes quickly once the conversation becomes black and white. In some circles, the debate between an Enemy-centric or Population-centric COIN strategy has become just that.[90]

Some leaders have taken extreme views supporting an enemy-focused strategy on the right or a population-focused strategy on the left. The debate is fueled by rigid views on either side. "COIN principles include changing our focus from killing and capturing insurgents to protecting the population and liberally funding economic development projects plus essential services."[91] Another one that captures attention is, "the American Army's new way of war, otherwise called Population-centric counterinsurgency, has become the only operational tool in the Army's repertoire to deal with the problems of insurgency and instability throughout the world."[92] The problem with statements such as these is they attempt to simplify and dumb down a very complex counterinsurgency effort. We have changed our focus from killing and capturing insurgents to relying on development and economic initiatives as the panacea for success? We only have the intellectual capacity to have one operational tool to deal with conflict?

These statements obviously represent the enemy-centric camp's portrayal of Population-centric strategies. They are far from the truth. The focus and importance of kill and capture operations in Afghanistan are not thrown into question just because there is more than one legitimate strategy available. Eliminating irreconcilable insurgents from the battlefield is a constant factor in any AO, no matter what the local commander wants to do.[93]

Enemy-focused strategy which seeks to attack the guerrilla forces directly risks dissipating effort in chasing insurgent groups all over the countryside, an activity that can be extremely demanding and requires enormous numbers of troops and other resources. Counterinsurgents who adopt this approach risk chasing their tails and so exhausting themselves, while doing enormous damage to the noncombatant civilian population, alienating the people and thus further strengthening their support for insurgency.[94]

The real trick for the commander is to evaluate whether kill or capture operations are the only option in his AO. If the insurgency is so fierce that kill or capture operations are the most viable course, then the commander must eliminate the insurgency. Next, he must accurately call the point at which his AO reaches a transition point so he can integrate other resources and assets as part of his strategy. Each area is different but there are always indicators to help commanders understand the complexity of their specific AOs.[95]

Once his AO achieves a transition point, the commander considers the assets at his disposal and which should be applied from across the lines of effort.[96] The same is true in reverse. If a commander's AO initially affords him the opportunity to apply multiple resources from across the lines of effort but the situation changes, he must detect it and be nimble enough to change course. If 200 insurgents enter the AO from across the border and enemy contact increases 200 percent, a precipitous change in strategy should follow. The key for the commander is not to indulge in rigid thinking. A balanced strategy is attained by the leader who understands which resources and assets are available, what the second and third order affect will be if he applies each one to his strategy, and to what percentage, if any at all, each asset can be applied in the first place. One senior commander stated, "A commander has to be able to do both [focus on the enemy and protect the population] and must have his hand on the thermostat and be able to dial it up and down based in the situation."[97] No cookie cutter solution or succinct combination of actions guarantees success. Afghanistan offers a mosaic of vastly different local environments and communities, each with its own unique history, traditions, and challenges.[98] Leaders who objectively reassess their local situations and adapt strategy to jive with their complex, ever-changing environments have the most likely shot at success.

The population-centric side of the argument contributed to fueling the debate in Afghanistan. In General McChrystal's initial counterinsurgency guidance issued on August 26th, 2009, it opened by stating, "The conflict will be won by persuading the population, not by destroying the enemy."[99] The ISAF mission statement itself directed its forces to conduct 'population-centric counterinsurgency' during this time. The concept was described through tactical directives but there was never a published definition of population-centric COIN. This oversight left some details open to interpretation by commanders on the ground; however, the author would argue the logic, intent, and desired end state were very clear from the start.[100]

Over the last couple years, the author has written a number of articles on how his squadron formulated and executed a balanced counterinsurgency strategy. The squadron referred to its strategy as population-centric. The infusion of development dollars, time with the locals and the trust and assistance earned from them over the course of deployment dovetailed with a sharp drop in violent attacks, enabling the Squadron feel to it had succeeded. Leaders chalked it up to the inclusion of population-centric strategy, rather than enemy-centric strategy in isolation. This, coupled with the fact that at the time of publishing these articles the ISAF mission statement directed a Population-centric approach, the author naturally titled the articles along the same lines. One of the articles was titled, "Implementing a Population Centric Strategy in Northeast Afghanistan, May 07 - July 08."[101] The intent was to demonstrate how the squadron achieved balance across the lines of effort in its AO by customizing those lines within each Troop AO based on the best route to defeat the insurgency. The use of the title term 'population-centric' to describe this complicated balancing act unfortunately cast this author as a "far left" thinker in some circles.[102] These circles contend subscribers to a population-centric strategy believe kill and capture operations are ineffective while development, essential services, and economy are the end-all, be-all utopia of counterinsurgency. That could not be further from the truth. Regardless, the author is guilty of contributing to this polarizing debate.

The author advocates for a balanced approach in which a commander is well resourced and bestowed the appropriate autonomy to apply assets across the lines of effort, tailored to his AO.[103] This balance and the application and weight of assets he applies, will fluctuate in each individual AO over time and will be intensely different across unit boundaries. The guiding strategy in Afghanistan from ISAF must allow for that autonomy and flexibility while clearly articulating the goals, glide path, and end state. The current ISAF guidance and mission statement do exactly that.[104]

The author has described the guiding strategy in Afghanistan using the analogy of a pendulum. For the first many years in Afghanistan, the strategy was heavily focused on enemy-centric, kill or capture operations. The coalition destroyed a huge number of insurgents and won every tactical engagement but created an equally astonishing number of converted insurgents because of civilian casualties and intrusive search, detainment, and interrogation practices. Then the pendulum swung the other way as ISAF led commanders to a population-centric strategy, which promoted partnering with and protecting the population against the insurgency, boosting their confidence, gaining their passive or active support, and utilizing all assets across the lines of effort to do so.

General Petraeus has made the final adjustment necessary to the guiding strategy at ISAF to give the coalition its best chance for success. He removed the term 'population-centric' from the mission statement, crystallized the ROE, and promoted the importance of a balanced strategy and each asset's potential impact on AOs. The mission statement reflects the balanced strategy necessary to attain a positive outcome in counterinsurgency operations in Afghanistan.[105] Neither an enemy, nor a population, nor an economic or development focused strategy will guarantee success in Afghanistan. A balanced approach in which we wisely deploy every asset in our arsenal as we listen to and protect the local population, support the government, build a competent and capable ANSF and aggressively pursue, capture or kill the enemy will.

Notes

1.   Oliver Roy, *Islam and Resistance in Afghanistan* (Cambridge, England: Cambridge University Press, 1990), 13

2.   Roy.

3.   Roy.

4.   Gilles Dorronsoro, *Revolution Unending: Afghanistan 1979 to the Present* (New York: Columbia University Press, 2005).

5.   Christopher Kolenda, "Command Brief," 1-91 CAV, 173rd Airborne," August 1, 2008, 9.

6.   Lester Grau and Ali Ahmad Jalali, *The Other Side of the Mountain: Mujahideen Tactics in the Soviet-Afghan War* (Quantico, Virginia: USMC Studies and Analysis Division, 1995), xi.

7.   It is important to note that the Soviets did not leave Afghanistan because of some military defeat as it is perceived sometimes in the West. There is no doubt that US-supplied weapons, especially surface to air systems, was an important factor in the Soviet decision to withdraw, but they were not beaten. In fact, According to Les Grau's book *The Other Side of the Mountain*, the Soviets lost 13,833 soldiers compared to the 1.3 million Afghan casualties. For as much as the Soviets did wrong, like the obvious slaughter of innocent civilians, they did a number of other things very well. They expertly trained the Afghan Security forces, discussed later in the chapter, and assisted the government to create a well functioning Communist system. As a result of these successes, the Afghan Communist government remained in power for two years after the Soviets withdrew.

8.   Daniel Marston, "Realizing the Extent of our Errors and Forging the Road Ahead," In *Counterinsurgency in Modern Warfare Second Edition*, ed. Daniel Marston et al. (Oxford: Osprey Publishing Company, 2010), 254-255.

9.   Dorronsoro, *Revolution Unending: Afghanistan 1979 to the Present*, 304-305.

10. Dorronsoro.

11. Antonio Giustozzi, *Empires of Mud: Wars and Warlords in Afghanistan* (New York: Columbia University Press, 2009), 89.

12. Christopher Kolenda, "Winning Afghanistan at the Community Level," *Joint Forces Quarterly* 56 (2010): 26-27.

13. The author subscribes to this theory as it best describes the effects of 30 years of war in N.E. Afghanistan where the author served as a commander. In Eastern Afghanistan, wealth was not assessed based upon how much money one possessed; rather, it was the size and breadth of possessions that mattered. Wealth was calculated in terms of volume. How much property did you have, compared to your neighbor, and how many heads of livestock? Was yours a large family?

These factors figured in heavily. The tribal system was not hierarchical, as the US military witnessed in Iraq. It was flat. Authority was localized and often didn't extend beyond the confines of the village or valley. The rich local level khans and elders established a dynasty of ruling power and wealth for generations of their families. In short, an individual's place in traditional society had more to do with who his father was than his potential or drive to succeed in life. For the lucky minority born into the rich families, this was great. For the rest, a life of hard labor and subsistence farming was about all one could expect. As mentioned above, each village or valley had a leader, a Khan, to lead a tribal style participatory democracy of elders and men in the area. Their regular meetings were called *jirgas*. They collectively hired a religious leader, a mullah, to serve their small populations. The mullah was usually paid by the community and under the authority of the Khan and elders. Thirty years of outside influence fragmented the traditional structure of Afghanistan's society. A new social order and opportunity presented itself. Money began to percolate into the country at unprecedented rates and created a new social mobility platform. New options abounded outside the traditional tribal structure for young men. History, family name, and social status did not dictate a man's future anymore and he no longer faced the once inevitable path of backbreaking subsistence farming. Now he had the option to join the resistance. The financial incentives were difficult to ignore, as was the sense of adventure. Each man had the opportunity to climb a new social mobility ladder that could potentially propel him to fame and fortune, especially if armed, while elevating his position, insuring a much better life for him and all who shared his table. For a generation of men, fighting has become a respected part of life in Afghanistan. It has illuminated a route out of extreme poverty and many previously hopeless men have hastened to take up arms as a means to a more successful life.

14. Kolenda, "Winning Afghanistan at the Community Level," 27.

15. John Malevich and Daryl Youngman, "The Afghan Balance of Power and the Culture of Jihad," *Military Review* (May-June 2011): 35.

16. Malevich and Youngman, 38.

17. Galula, Counterinsurgency Warfare: Theory and Practice, 95.

18. United Nations Security Council, "Agreement on Provincial Arrangements in Afghanistan Pending the Re-Establishment of Permanent Government Institutions," Security Council Resolution (S/2001/1154): 2-8.

19. Kenneth Katzman, RL30588, *Afghanistan: Post-Taliban Governance, Security, and US Policy,* Washington, DC: Congressional Research Service, 11.

20. Katzman., 12.

21. There were plenty of units that adopted a unique approach that was adapted to their individual AOs integrating all lines of effort. The approach was anything but conventional wisdom at the time. It would be ridiculous to say commanders across Afghanistan weren't creating vastly different approaches to accommodate their local conditions. The execution of the ISAF strategy was

anything but black and white and did have an important component attached to it and that was autonomy. Individual commanders did have the autonomy to deviate from conventional wisdom. Still, the focus at the top in ISAF was heavily focused on the enemy. As the surge of soldiers is complete in Afghanistan today, the numbers have drastically increased. According to the ISAF website, the total troop numbers in Afghanistan as of May 16, 2011 are approximately 90,000 US soldiers and an additional 42,400 ISAF soldiers from 47 contributing countries. The total number of ISAF soldiers in Afghanistan is 132,400.

22. Amy Belasco, RL33110, *The Cost of Iraq, Afghanistan, and Other Global War On Terror Operations Since 9/11* (Washington, DC: Congressional Research Service, March 29, 2011), 44-45.

23. International Security and Assistance Force Command., "Mission Statement.," Website. http://www.isaf.nato.int/mission.html (accessed May 18, 2011). The increase in combat maneuver Brigades in Afghanistan between 2002 and now is dramatic. In 2002, there were 2 US maneuver brigades in country. According to the ISAF website as of 18 May, 2011, there are 13 US maneuver brigades in country and that is not counting Provincial Reconstruction Teams and detached battalions.

24. Frank Kitson, *Low Intensity Operations* (London, Faber and Faber Publishing, 1971), 200.

25. Kitson, 200-201.

26. Stanley McChrystal, "ISAF Counterinsurgency Training Guidance." Kabul, AF: International Security and Assistance Force, November 10, 2009.

27. There are 48 ISAF contributing countries including the United States as of May 2011. Each nation has different national laws dictating what military roles and responsibilities they can and cannot contribute to the war effort in Afghanistan. Formulating a strategic theater level strategy that maximizes each nation's potential contribution taking into account the caveats is difficult.

28. John Nagl, "A Better War in Afghanistan: Senate Committee on Foreign Relations," *Center for New American Security* (September 16, 2009): 4.

29. William Caldwell and Steven Leonard, "Field Manual 3-07, Stability Operations: Upshifting the Engine of Change," *Military Review 88* (July/August 2008), 6.

30. BA090, Brigade Commander, Interview by Mark Battjes and Benjamin Boardman, 24 February 2011, Fort Riley, KS.

31. BA080, Counterinsurgency Advisor, Interview by Richard Johnson and Nathan Springer, 9 March 2011, Fort Leavenworth, KS.

32. BE090, Battalion Commander, Interview by Robert Green and Aaron Kaufman, 7 March 2011, Fort Irwin, CA.

33. Marston, "Realizing the Extent of our Errors and Forging the Road Ahead," 261.

34. David McKiernan, "Counterinsurgency guidance paper," (Kabul, AF: International Security and Assistance Force, March 18, 2009), 2.

35. BH040, Afghanistan Veterans Panel. Interview by Richard Johnson, Aaron Kaufman, Nathan Springer, and Thomas Walton, 24 March 2011, Quantico, VA.

36. Much of the COIN guidance that was created under General McKiernan was adopted, adapted, and implemented by General Mchrystal when he took command in 2009.

37. Laura Rozen, "Winning hearts and minds: all of McChrystal's advisors," *Foreign Policy,* July 31, 2009. http://thecable.foreignpolicy.com/posts/2009/07/31/ winning_hearts_and_minds_all_of_mcchrystals_advisors. (accessed May 8, 2011).

38. Stanley McChrystal, "Commander's Initial Assessment," (Kabul, AF: International Security and Assistance Force, August 30, 2009), 1-2.

39. McChrystal, 1-9. The population-centric COIN directive intended to focus ISAF units on the population and not just the enemy was successful in most areas but had a negative effect on the force in some units. Other units adapted their operations to meet the ISAF commander's intent in a way that remained appropriate to their unique local conditions and the strength of the insurgency. This is discussed in detail later in the chapter.

40. Information briefing conducted at the ISAF T3C counterinsurgency academy in Kabul, AF on March 18, 2010 witnessed by the author.

41. Stanley McChrystal, "Tactical Directive," (Kabul, AF: International Security and Assistance Force, July 6, 2009) 1-2.

42. When General Petraeus took over in July 2010 he changed very little that General McChrystal had set in motion as the new strategy in Afghanistan. He agreed with almost everything. The one thing that the Petraeus team did change was the ISAF mission statement and the use of the term population-centric COIN and cleared up the ROE regarding indirect fire and CAS. As described, the term was used by General McChrystal to signal a transition at the time and convey the importance of partnering with and protecting the population and not simply focusing on the enemy. Over time, some leaders at levels below ISAF began to see the directive as black and white, creating additional measures to enforce and comply with it, which made the rules of engagement in some units more rigid. The Petraeus team recognized this, removed the term population-centric, and changed the mission statement to simply read 'conduct operations in Afghanistan.'

43. McChrystal, "Tactical Directive," 2.

44. ROE regarding the use of Indirect Fire and CAS would be reviewed by General Petraeus in July 2010. Although he would not change the directive issued by General McChrystal, he would issue guidance to ensure leaders at all levels understood the appropriate use. This is discussed in the following pages at length.

45. McChrystal, "Tactical Directive," 2.

46. Sean Naylor and Michael Hoffman, "Petraeus Reviews, clarifies strike directive," Air Force Times, August 9, 2010. http://www.airforcetimes.com/ news/2010/08/ airforce_rules_of_engagement_080910/. (accessed 18 May 2011).

47. This information was obtained at the unclassified level while attending the Afghan Counterinsurgency Academy at Camp Julien, Afghanistan in March 2010. General McChrystal laid out the goals for the ANSF calling it a critical component to the strategy and overall success in Afghanistan.

48. McChrystal, "Commander's Initial Assessment," G-1.

49. Coupled with the desperate need to immediately amplify the recruiting, vetting, and training of the ANSF is the importance of effective partnership. One key obstacle to our training efforts in Afghanistan is patience. No one has uncovered a shortcut to building an elite force. It takes time to grow and develop leaders, which is integral to establishing a viable Security Force. In the US Army, the average battalion commander logs between 16 and 18 years of experience before assuming command. In Afghanistan today, Commands are purchased rather than earned. As the ANSF ranks swell, the risk of a leadership crisis looms on the horizon, threatening to unseat the delicate balance of order. One-to-one partnership with ANSF forces is more critical today than ever before and, since 2009, it has become a high priority at every level. One US Commander acknowledged the importance of one-to-one partnering in his AO stating "ANSF capacity-building is our main effort, and we accept some risk in our operational capabilities to focus on this." (Steven Bowman and Catherine Dale, *War in Afghanistan: Strategy, Military Operations, and Issues for Congress,* 47) Make no mistake, an efficient and well functioning Afghan National Security Force will predicate a successful ISAF withdrawal in the coming years.

50. Katzman, "Afghanistan: Post-Taliban Governance, Security, and US Policy," 26.

51. Katzman, 26.

52. The White House, "Remarks by the President in Address to the Nation on the Way Forward in Afghanistan and Pakistan," The White House, Office of the Press Secretary, December 1, 2009.

53. Naylor and Hoffman, "Petraeus Reviews, clarifies strike directive," accessed May 18, 2011.

54. ISAF, "Mission Statement," *International Security and Assistance Force Command Website,* 2011. http://www.isaf.nato.int/mission.html (accessed May 2, 2011).

55. Sana Haroon, *Frontier of Faith: Islam in the Indo-Afghan Borderland* (New York: Columbia University Press, 2007), 16.

56. BB020, Battalion Commander, Interview by Mark Battjes and Nathan Springer, March 2, 2011, Fort Bliss, TX.

57. Roy, *Islam and Resistance in Afghanistan*, 10.

58. Malevich and Youngman, "The Afghan Balance of Power and the Culture of Jihad," 35.

59. Marston, "Realizing the Extent of our Errors and Forging the Road Ahead," 252.

60. Kolenda, "Winning Afghanistan at the Community Level," 29.

61. A tribal *jirga* was defined as a meeting among the men and elders within a village or valley in order to decide on local governance matters and decisions that affected the community. This is opposed to a *shura*, which would have the religious Mullahs of the area in attendance. *Shuras* had a religious component or a decision was involved that was associated with religion. The unit was corrected many times by elders in the local communities in the AO when asked to hold a *shura*. Leaders would share a laugh and they would correct the terminology each time and say, 'you mean you want to have a *jirga*'!

62. Nathan Springer, "Implementing a Population-centric Strategy in Northeast Afghanistan, May 07-July 08." *Small Wars Journal,* March 1st, 2010. http://smallwarsjournal.com/blog/2010/03/   implementing-a-populationcentr/. (accessed May 2, 2011).

63. Dorronsoro, *Revolution Unending: Afghanistan 1979 to the Present,* 329-334.

64. Roy, *Islam and Resistance in Afghanistan*, 20-21.

65. Rhoda Margesson, R40747, "United Nations Assistance Mission in Afghanistan: Background and Policy Issues," *Congressional Research Service.* December 27, 2010, 18.

66. Nagl, "A Better War in Afghanistan: Senate Committee on Foreign Relations," 8.

67. Kolenda, "Winning Afghanistan at the Community Level," 30.

68. McChrystal, "Commander's Initial Assessment," 2-9.

69. Katzman, "Afghanistan: Post-Taliban Governance, Security, and US Policy," 12.

70. Interview with BB020, March 2, 2011, Fort Bliss, TX.

71. Interview with BB020, March 2, 2011, Fort Bliss, TX.

72. Interview with BB020, March 2, 2011, Fort Bliss, TX.

73. Kolenda, "Command Brief," August 1, 2008.

74. Much of the literature alludes to ungoverned space. There is no such thing. Governance is the traditional system in place or power broker in a village, valley, or area that administers the rules and regulations while enforcing the traditional customs and way of life. Government is more formal. The first hint of government comes at the district level in Afghanistan and extends to the provincial

and central levels. Formal government is often mistrusted by the locals because of a history of corruption and falsehood. Governance has functioned for centuries in Afghanistan while government has not. We must connect the government with the functioning governance to set the conditions for peace, self-reliance, and progress in the future.

75. Margesson, "United Nations Assistance Mission in Afghanistan: Background and Policy Issues," 9.

76. Jerry Meyerle, Megan Katt, and Jim Gavrilis, CRM D0022894.A2, "Counterinsurgency on the Ground in Afghanistan: How different units adapted to local conditions," Center of Navy Analysis, July 1, 2010, 51-64.

77. Kolenda, "Command Brief," August 1, 2008.

78. Meyerle, Katt, and Gavrilis, "Counterinsurgency on the Ground in Afghanistan: How different units adapted to local conditions," 53-54.

79. Craig Collier, "Now That We're Leaving Iraq, What Did We Learn," *Military Review* (September-October 2010): 91.

80. Meyerle, Katt, and Gavrilis, "Counterinsurgency on the Ground in Afghanistan: How different units adapted to local conditions," 55-57.

81. Joseph Cox, "Information Operations in Operation Enduring Freedom and Operation Iraqi Freedom – What Went Wrong" (Monograph, School of Advanced Military Studies: Fort Leavenworth, 2006), 39.

82. Information briefing conducted at the ISAF T3C counterinsurgency academy in Kabul, AF on March 18, 2010 witnessed by the author. Although the RIB program officially began in 2006, radio stations were being procured prior to that year by individual commands. Once the program became standardized in 2006, it functioned better nationally as radio station components were standardized.

83. Interview with BI050, March 28, 2011, United Kingdom.

84. In Northeast Konar and Eastern Nuristan Province in 2007 and 2008, the 1st Squadron, 91st Cavalry stretched this concept as far as it could to extract as much benefit as possible. At Forward Operating Base Naray, 1-91 purchased an FM radio station that had an increased range due to repeaters. Thousands of wind-up radios were distributed to the local population and the radio station broadcast in Pashtun and Nuristani 18 hours a day by an all Afghan staff. Additionally, an all Afghan run newspaper was published weekly at Naray. It reported positive news and human interest stories, as well as local tribal news. The paper was distributed to every major village in the area of operation and provided an excellent avenue for informing locals of our efforts in their area. The other important function the Afghan newspaper staff performed was the creation of flyers for use prior to and during tactical operations. The funding to maintain the radio station and newspaper was made available through a combination of funding mechanisms including CERP, local area contract, and battalion funds. The information

operations effort was a critical component to the overall strategy.

85. Spencer Ackerman, "Military Embraces Counterinsurgency in Afghanistan," *The Washington Independent,* September 29, 2008. http:// washingtonindependent.com/8821/ counterinsurgency-in-afghanistan. (accessed May 19, 2011).

86. Greg Bruno, "Winning the Information War in Afghanistan and Pakistan," *Council on Foreign Relations*, May 11, 2009. http://www.cfr.org/ pakistan/winning-information-war-afghanistan-pakistan/p19330 (accessed April 30, 2011).

87. Malevich and Youngman, "The Afghan Balance of Power and the Culture of Jihad," 38.

88. Malevich and Youngman, 39.

89. For more information regarding the debate on religion in Afghanistan read Oliver Roy's book *Islam and Resistance in Afghanistan* and Sana Haroon's book, *Frontier of Faith.*

90. To see how this debate has gripped our military, read Binard Finel's "A substitute for Victory," in *Foreign Affairs* April 8, 2010 that supports population-centric COIN as the strategy in Afghanistan and Colonel Gian Gentile's "A Strategy of Tactics: Population-centric COIN and the Army," in *Parameters,* Autumn 2009 that disapproves of the strategy.

91. Collier, "Now That We're Leaving Iraq, What Did We Learn," 88.

92. Gian Gentile, "A Strategy of Tactics: Population-centric COIN and the Army," *Parameters* (Autumn 2009): 6.

93. Interview with BH040, 24 March 2011, Quantico, VA.

94. Kilcullen, *Counterinsurgency*, 9.

95. Andrew Knight, "Influence as a Measure of Success," *Military Review* (January-February 2011): 71.

96. Lines of effort include but are not limited to: Security (which includes Kill / Capture Operations and ANSF, Economy, Development, Governance, and Information Operations / Psychological Operations.

97. BB030, Brigade Commander. Interview by Mark Battjes and Nathan Springer, 3 March 2011, Fort Bliss, TX.

98. Marston, "Realizing the Extent of our Errors and Forging the Road Ahead," 285.

99. Stanley McChrystal, "ISAF Commander's Counterinsurgency Guidance," *International Security Assistance Force,* August 26, 2009.

100. From May 2007 to July 2008 in Afghanistan, 1-91 Cavalry Squadron focused on partnering with and protecting the population from the insurgency in the AO. The Squadron was in the AO for two summer fighting periods, which

is rare, and it makes for a good case study. The precipitous drop in violence the Squadron experienced between the first and second summer was dramatic.

101. Nathan Springer, "Implementing a Population-centric Strategy in Northeast Afghanistan, May 07-July 08." *Small Wars Journal*, March 1st, 2010, http://smallwarsjournal.com/blog/2010/03/implementing-a-populationcentr/, (accessed May 2, 2011).

102. The author has written a number of articles on this experience using the term population-centric to describe the strategy. They are: "Taking the Next Step: Operationalizing a Population-Centric Strategy at the Battalion-Squadron Level," US Army and Marine Corps Counterinsurgency Center, January 11, 2010; "Isolating the Critical Element Necessary to Achieve Success in a Population Centric Environment: Close Personal Relationships," US Army and Marine Corps Counterinsurgency Center, March 1, 2010, and "Many Paths Up the Mountain: Population Centric COIN in Afghanistan, " Small Wars Journal, May 25, 2010.

103. Balanced approach: This does not mean that a commander utilized all assets equally. The commander must understand which assets are available, consider each one across every line of effort, and apply them in proportions that best address local conditions.

104. ISAF, "Mission Statement," *International Security and Assistance Force Command Website,* 2011. http://www.isaf.nato.int/mission.html (accessed May 2, 2011).

105. ISAF, "Mission Statement".

Chapter 6

Conclusion

The debate over population-centric versus enemy-centric compartmentalizes our thinking and it's not an either or proposition. . . . Those are not mutually exclusive but I think the emotion gets up and people wind up justifying their position at the expense of relevance and reality. I honestly think it stifles some of the things that we are really trying to do. . . . I think we have to be cautious of that because there are assumptions built in to labels like that when quite frankly they have to be applied differently every single place we go.

— BA060, Counterinsurgency Advisor,
Fort Leavenworth, KS

The case studies suggest that commanders who craft a balanced strategy integrating all resources while simultaneously shielding civilians and conducting aggressive, intelligence-driven offensive operations, most frequently encounter success in their AOs. The polarizing debate over whether to employ a population-centric or enemy-centric strategy to achieve superior victory in a counterinsurgency campaign became complicated because each side is partially correct. AOs benefit from enemy elimination, absolutely. AOs benefit from civilians who feel safe and protected from the insurgency but a purely population-centric or enemy-centric counterinsurgency approach exists mostly in theory and, in practice, it can leave gaping deficits in strategy. The key is to accept there are no black or white solutions when countering an insurgency. Appropriate solutions depend on unique factors, inherent to local areas. These AOs require creative applications of available resources from across the lines of effort to best combat the insurgency and improve local conditions.

Commanders at the operational and strategic levels must acknowledge this and issue guidance that delivers clearly articulated goals and milestones. It must point the desired way ahead, such as General Briggs did when he took over as director of operations in Malaya in 1950.[1]

It must illuminate the path to a political solution while allowing junior commanders at the tactical level the necessary autonomy to formulate and execute the unique day-to-day strategy necessary to move AOs to agreed upon end states. Every asset available to leaders across the lines of effort must be considered when formulating their individual plans for their AOs. The case studies which the essay has examined show the complexity of the debate and the need for nuanced understanding.

The physical act of war begins with, is connected to, and ends with a political solution. The theorists in chapter 2, whether conventional war theorists or more contemporary counterinsurgency theorists, agree that to achieve an acceptable solution in war, every applicable element of national power must be applied in the conflict to integrate and synchronize the effort that enables the quickest political resolution or settlement.[2] How the available elements of national power are weighted when applied to the war, whether offensive operations or governance, diplomacy, development, or economic initiatives, are contingent upon dynamics on the ground. The theorists would never dismiss a potential resource, asset, or opportunity available to them that could be applied to the war effort and potentially contribute to reaching a political solution. It was apparent to them that the solutions in war that prompt political negotiation or compromise are often gray and require constant evaluation and manipulation; no one cookie-cutter paradigm fits all.[3]

The counterinsurgency campaigns in both Malaya and Oman demonstrate that if a strategy is too focused on killing and capturing the enemy or favors the population to the exclusion of enemy, progress is slow. Contrary to current US military conventional wisdom, Malaya was not a population-centric campaign. In fact, it was not centric at all. While the scale of the British government's national power application was vastly different in both campaigns, similar lessons emerged. Malaya was highly organized and well resourced while Oman was decentralized and under resourced. In both campaigns, it took flexibility, time, and adaptation by leaders at all levels to achieve a balanced strategy. Offensive operations started out enemy-centric, heavily focused on killing or capturing insurgents. While the approach brought limited success, it did so with a high number of associated civilian casualties pushing popular support toward the insurgents. As leaders developed a more nuanced understanding of their respective insurgencies, the strategy became more balanced.

Offensive operations better utilized intelligence to target the enemy. Resources were leveraged from across the lines of effort both in support of the population and against the insurgency. Economic and development initiatives were utilized in government-controlled areas to reinforce gains and incentivize further cooperation and support from the population. Life began to look better under government control rather than insurgent control. Population control measures were utilized against the insurgency. In Malaya, even with a long list of associated issues, resettlement and food control denied the insurgency access to the local Chinese population in the jungle.[4] In Dhofar, Oman, villages were secured by physical barriers that controlled access, necessarily isolating the insurgency from the population. Construction of a series of blocking obstacles greatly degraded the Adoo's ability to resupply its forces from PDRY.[5] Offensive operations continued in both campaigns. The balanced approach, utilizing every available resource in support of government forces and against the insurgency, illuminated the brightest path to political reconciliation.

The case studies on Malaya and Oman are informative to our current conflict in Afghanistan. For a large portion of the conflict the coalition was heavily focused on enemy-centric, large scale offensive operations. Although there were units at the tactical level pursuing unique balanced approaches conducive to the local situations they faced, the strategy at the operational level remained focused on killing and capturing insurgents until 2009.[6] To complicate matters, by 2003, American war attention and resources were diverted to Iraq and the war effort in Afghanistan was secondary to the war effort in Iraq until 2009. Everything, from resources to the total number of soldiers committed to the conflict, was done on the cheap. All elements of national power were hardly committed against the insurgency in Afghanistan.

In 2009, President Obama officially shifted the focus of the US war effort from Iraq to Afghanistan. General McChrystal adjusted the ISAF approach from an enemy-centric to a population-centric one. He guided the force to partner with and protect the population, he doubled efforts to train, mentor, and partner with the ANSF, and he better focused the effort to kill and capture the enemy. Between 2009 and 2010, ISAF directed an effort to utilize all resources and elements of national power against the insurgency, with particular emphasis on avoiding civilian casualties. Although the intent was to balance the strategy, the population-centric directive swung the pendulum too far the other way. In the spirit of complying with the directive, some commanders added additional restrictions to protect the population that made the rules of engagement (ROE) more rigid, which constrained some units when trying to integrate critical assets such as close air support or fires while engaged with the enemy. As a retired general officer concluded, "There has to be a degree of caution [to prevent civilian casualties and increase popular support] but you must ensure you [your directives] don't have unnecessary caution as you can quickly border, frankly, on pacifism."[7]

General David Petraeus took command of ISAF in July of 2010 and continued General McChrystal's strategy but removed the population-centric directive from the ISAF mission statement. Petraeus issued a directive preventing commanders from adding additional restrictions to the ROE. Petraeus made small adjustments to the strategy; however, in doing so he created a more balanced approach. ISAF now promotes a strategy that recognizes the importance of every available resource and the complexity of each local area. Commanders at the tactical level have the autonomy to create and execute strategies they feel will work best in their AOs while staying true to their senior commanders' intent. ISAF has placed itself in a promising position to induce a political solution in the future as all resources are applied at varying but seemingly appropriate levels across Afghanistan.

In closing, counterinsurgency strategy should not be categorized in mutually exclusive terms such as population-centric or enemy-centric because countering insurgents requires a far more dynamic, hybrid approach. The US military, strategists, and policy makers must retire the "centric" narrative and work together to integrate and utilize every available resource as part of a balanced approach. Counterinsurgency strategy planning requires a nimble and expansive mindset. We must understand that counterinsurgency is simply one more type of warfare and one that we are sure to experience again. The careful analysis of current and future counterinsurgency campaigns must first start with history. The best practices, hard lessons, and recommended solutions history provides us both highlight the starting point and illuminate the way ahead from which to navigate uncharted waters. Military commanders, strategists, and policy makers must analyze historical campaigns in depth and avoid cherry picking history for the sake of their arguments. The critical lesson that bound to the fore from the case studies in this thesis was that success demands a balanced approach in counterinsurgency that aggressively pursues the enemy while at the same time partners with and protects the population.

Notes

1. For more information on General Briggs four main aims to improve the counterinsurgency effort in Mayala, read page 52 in chapter 3 on Malaya.

2. Sun Tzu, *The Art of War* (London: Oxford University Press, 1963), 39.

3. For further examination of the war theorists and the potential approaches in war to win, achieve political compromise, or negotiated settlement, please read chapter two of this thesis. Theorists analyzed in the chapter include classic theorists such as Suz-Tzu, Jomini, and Clausewitz; insurgent theorists Mao Tse-Tung and Giap; and counterinsurgency theorists Julian Paget, Frank Kitson, Robert Thompson, Roger Trinquier, David Galula, John McCuen, David Kilcullen, John Mackinlay.

4. As shown in the Malaya chapter, resettlement of the local Chinese population in the jungle was anything but smooth in the beginning. Resettlement villages lacked basic services and were unhealthy and dangerous to live in. It took a concerted effort on behalf of the British and Malay government to improve resettlement centers, add essential services, and create acceptable living conditions.

5. For more information on the population control measures employed against the insurgency in Malaya and Dhofar province, Oman, see chapter 3 and 4.

6. This issue becomes much more nebulous at the tactical level. Afghanistan was the war of secondary importance to Iraq from 2003 to 2009 and a small number of units were operating in Afghanistan as compared to Iraq. This made areas of operation at the company, battalion, and brigade level in Afghanistan very large, which afforded commanders great autonomy to apply solutions they deemed most appropriate to their individual AOs. There were commanders and units applying balanced approaches conducive to their local AOs between 2002 and 2009. The issue is that the lack of guidance at the strategic and operational levels afforded other commanders the opportunity to pursue an enemy-centric strategy in their AOs even if a balanced strategy was more appropriate. The lack of higher guidance makes autonomy your best friend and worst enemy at the same time.

7. Interview with BI070, 30 March 2011, United Kingdom.

Bibliography

Primary Sources

Interviews

Command and General Staff College (CGSC) Scholars Program 2011. Scholars Program *Counterinsurgency Research Study 2011*. Research Study, Fort Leavenworth, KS: Ike Skelton Chair in Counterinsurgency, 2011. This study included interviews of counterinsurgency practitioners and policy professionals from the United States and United Kingdom. All interviews are held with the Ike Skelton Chair in Counterinsurgency, CGSC Fort Leavenworth, KS.

Boston, Massachusetts

BF010, Former Army Officer. Interview by Richard Johnson and Aaron Kaufman, 11 March 2011.

BF020, Civilian Advisor to MNF-I. Interview by Richard Johnson and Aaron Kaufman, 11 March 2011.

BF030, Battery Commander. Interview by Richard Johnson and Aaron Kaufman, 12 March 2011.

BF040, Battery Commander. Interview by Richard Johnson and Aaron Kaufman, 14 March 2011.

Fort Bliss, Texas

BB010, Battalion Commander. Interview by Mark Battjes and Nathan Springer, 2 March 2011.

BB020, Battalion Commander. Interview by Mark Battjes and Nathan Springer, 2 March 2011.

BB030, Brigade Commander. Interview by Mark Battjes and Nathan Springer, 3 March 2011.

Fort Bragg, North Carolina

BC010, Field Grade Officer. Interview by Robert Green and Aaron Kaufman, 1 March 2011.

BC020, Brigade Commander. Interview by Robert Green and Aaron Kaufman, 2 March 2011.

BC030, Battalion Commander. Interview by Benjamin Boardman and Richard Johnson, 1 March 2011.

BC040, Battalion Commander. Interview by Benjamin Boardman and Richard Johnson, 2 March 2011.

BC050, Battalion Commander. Interview by Benjamin Boardman and Richard Johnson, 2 March 2011.

BC060, Battalion Commander. Interview by Benjamin Boardman and Richard Johnson, 3 March 2011.

Fort Irwin, California

BE010, Transition Team Leader. Interview by Mark Battjes and Thomas Walton, 7 March 2011.

BE020, Transition Team Member. Interview by Mark Battjes and Thomas Walton, 7 March 2011.

BE030, Company Commander. Interview by Mark Battjes and Thomas Walton, 8 March 2011.

BE040, Transition Team Leader. Interview by Mark Battjes and Thomas Walton, 9 March 2011.

BE050, Battery Commander. Interview by Robert Green and Aaron Kaufman, 8 March 2011.

BE060, Brigade Commander. Interview by Mark Battjes and Thomas Walton, 9 March 2011.

BE070, Field Grade Officer. Interview by Robert Green and Aaron Kaufman, 9 March 2011.

BE080, Battalion Commander. Interview by Robert Green and Aaron Kaufman, 7 March 2011.

BE090, Battalion Commander. Interview by Robert Green and Aaron Kaufman, 7 March 2011.

Fort Knox, Kentucky

BD010, Field Grade Officer. Interview by Benjamin Boardman and Dustin Mitchell, 14 March 2011.

BD020, Commander. Interview by Benjamin Boardman and Dustin Mitchell, 14 March 2011.

BD030, Commander. Interview by Benjamin Boardman and Dustin Mitchell, 14 March 2011.

BD040, Commander. Interview by Benjamin Boardman and Dustin Mitchell, 15 March 2011.

BD050, Commander. Interview by Benjamin Boardman and Dustin Mitchell, 15 March 2011.

BD060, Field Grade Officer. Interview by Benjamin Boardman and Dustin Mitchell, 16 March 2011.

BD070, Field Grade Officer. Interview by Benjamin Boardman and Dustin Mitchell, 16 March 2011.

BD080, Field Grade Officer. Interview by Benjamin Boardman and Dustin Mitchell, 17 March 2011.

Fort Leavenworth, Kansas

BA010, Brigade Commander. Interview by Richard Johnson and Thomas Walton, 22 February 2011.

BA020, Battalion Commander. Interview by Mark Battjes and Benjamin Boardman, 23 February 2011.

BA030, Vietnam Veteran. Interview by Aaron Kaufman and Dustin Mitchell, 24 February 2011.

BA040, Brigade Commander. Interview by Aaron Kaufman and Dustin Mitchell, 23 February, 2011.

BA050, Battalion Commander. Interview by Robert Green and Nathan Springer, 23 February, 2011.

BA060, Counterinsurgency Advisor. Interview by Robert Green and Nathan Springer, 23 February, 2011.

BA070, Battery Commander. Interview by Richard Johnson and Thomas Walton, 24 February 2011.

BA080, Counterinsurgency Advisor. Interview by Richard Johnson and Nathan Springer, 9 March 2011.

BA090, Brigade Commander. Interview by Mark Battjes and Benjamin Boardman, 24 February 2011.

Fort Stewart, Georgia

BG020, Brigade Commander. Interview by Mark Battjes and Thomas Walton, 14 March 2011.

BG030, Troop Commander. Interview by Mark Battjes, Nathan Springer, and Thomas Walton, 14 March 2011.

BG040, Brigade Commander. Interview by Nathan Springer and Thomas Walton, 15 March 2011.

BG050, Battalion Commander. Interview by Mark Battjes, 15 March 2011.

BG060, Battalion Commander. Interview by Mark Battjes, 15 March 2011.

BG070, Field Grade Officer. Interview by Nathan Springer and Thomas Walton, 15 March 2011.

BG080, Battalion Commander. Interview by Mark Battjes and Thomas Walton, 16 March 2011.

BG090, Battalion Commander. Interview by Mark Battjes and Nathan Springer, 16 March 2011.

BG100, Brigade Commander. Interview by Mark Battjes and Nathan Springer, 16 March 2011.

United Kingdom

BI010, Senior British Officer. Interview by Mark Battjes, Benjamin Boardman, Robert Green, Richard Johnson, Aaron Kaufman, Dustin Mitchell, and Nathan Springer, 29 March 2011.

BI020, Battle Group Commander. Interview by Aaron Kaufman and Thomas Walton, 31 March 2011.

BI030, Field Grade Officer. Interview by Robert Green and Thomas Walton, 29 March 2011.

BI040, Field Grade Officer. Interview by Mark Battjes and Dustin Mitchell, 1 April 2011.

BI050, Dhofar Veterans Panel. Interview by Mark Battjes, Benjamin Boardman, Robert Green, Richard Johnson, Aaron Kaufman, Dustin Mitchell, Nathan Springer, and Thomas Walton, 28 March 2011.

BI060, Dhofar Veterans Panel. Interview by Interview by Mark Battjes, Benjamin Boardman, Robert Green, Richard Johnson, Aaron Kaufman, Dustin Mitchell, Nathan Springer, and Thomas Walton, 2 April 2011.

BI070, Retired General Officer. Interview by Interview by Mark Battjes, Benjamin Boardman, Robert Green, Richard Johnson, Aaron Kaufman, Dustin Mitchell, Nathan Springer, and Thomas Walton, 30 March 2011.

BI080, Retired General Officer. Interview by Benjamin Boardman, Robert Green, Nathan Springer, and Thomas Walton, 3 April 2011.

BI090, Retired General Officer. Interview by Benjamin Boardman, Robert Green, Nathan Springer, and Thomas Walton, 4 April 2011.

BI100, Senior Army Officer. Interview by Mark Battjes, Richard Johnson, Aaron Kaufman, and Dustin Mitchell, 4 April 2011.

BI110, Battalion Commander. Interview by Mark Battjes, Richard Johnson, and Dustin Mitchell, 8 April 2011.

BI120, Retired Army Officer. Interview by Benjamin Boardman, Robert Green, Nathan Springer, and Thomas Walton, 8 April 2011.

BI130, Platoon Commander. Interview by Benjamin Boardman and Richard Johnson, 5 April 2011.

BI140, Afghan Army Advisor. Interview by Benjamin Boardman and Richard Johnson, 5 April 2011.

BI150, Company Sergeant Major. Interview by Aaron Kaufman and Dustin Mitchell, 5 April 2011.

BI160, Company Second In Command. Interview by Aaron Kaufman and Dustin Mitchell, 5 April 2011.

BI170, Afghan Army Advisor. Interview by Aaron Kaufman and Dustin Mitchell, 5 April 2011.

BI190, Senior Non-Commissioned Officer. Interview by Mark Battjes and Thomas Walton, 5 April 2011.

BI200, Platoon Commander. Interview by Aaron Kaufman and Dustin Mitchell, 7 April 2011.

BI210, Company 2nd In Command. Interview by Mark Battjes and Thomas Walton, 7 April 2011.

BI220, Field Grade Officer. Interview by Aaron Kaufman and Dustin Mitchell, 7 April 2011.

BI230, Company Commander. Interview by Robert Green and Nathan Springer, 7 April 2011.

BI240, Company Grade Officer. Interview by Benjamin Boardman and Richard Johnson, 7 April 2011.

BI250, Battalion Commander. Interview by Benjamin Boardman and Richard Johnson, 7 April 2011.

BI260, Non-Commissioned Officer. Interview by Robert Green and Nathan Springer, 7 April 2011.

BI270, Company Grade Officer. Interview by Mark Battjes and Thomas Walton, 7 April 2011.

BI280, Commander's Panel. Interview by Richard Johnson, 1 April 2011.

BI290, Battery Commander. Interview by Richard Johnson, 1 April 2011.

BI300, Company Commander. Interview by Richard Johnson, 2 April 2011.

BI310, Company Commander. Interview by Benjamin Boardman and Nathan Springer, 31 March 2011.

BI320, Field Grade Officer. Interview by Benjamin Boardman and Dustin Mitchell, 29 March 2011.

BI330, Dhofar Veteran. Interview by Robert Green, 28 March 2011.

Washington, DC

BH010, Senior Policy Official. Interview by Mark Battjes, Benjamin Boardman, Robert Green, Richard Johnson, Aaron Kaufman, Dustin Mitchell, Nathan Springer, and Thomas Walton, 21 March 2011.

BH020, Field Grade Officer. Interview by Mark Battjes, Benjamin Boardman, Robert Green, Richard Johnson, Aaron Kaufman, Dustin Mitchell, Nathan Springer, and Thomas Walton, 21 March 2011.

BH030, Iraq Veterans Panel. Interview by Mark Battjes, Robert Green, Aaron Kaufman, and Dustin Mitchell, 22 March 2011.

BH040, Afghanistan Veterans Panel. Interview by Richard Johnson, Aaron Kaufman, Nathan Springer, and Thomas Walton, 24 March 2011.

BH050, Historian. Interview by Mark Battjes, Robert Green, Richard Johnson, Aaron Kaufman, and Dustin Mitchell, 22 March 2011.

BH060, Vietnam Political and Military Analyst. Interview by Mark Battjes, Benjamin Boardman, Robert Green, and Dustin Mitchell, 22 March 2011.

BH070, Iraqi Mayor. Interview by Mark Battjes and Robert Green, 25 March 2011.

Personal Accounts

Akehurst, John. *We Won A War: The Campaign in Oman 1965-1975.* Southhampton, England: Camelot Press Ltd, 1982.

Corum, James. "Training Indigenous Forces in Counterinsurgency: A Tale of Two Insurgencies." Monograph, Strategic Studies Institute, National War College, 2006.

Collier, Craig. "Now that we're leaving Iraq, what did we learn." *Military Review* (September-October 2010): 88-93.

Cox, Joseph. "Information Operations in Operation Enduring Freedom and Operation Iraqi Freedom – What Went Wrong." Monograph, School of Advanced Military Studies: Fort Leavenworth, AY 05-06)

Dhofar Veteran Manuscript, "Dhofar 1970-1980 a Briefing: A ten year progress from PSYOPS to a Ministry of Information," March 28, 2011.

Galula, David. *Counterinsurgency Warfare: Theory and Practice.* Westport, CT: Praegar Security International, 2006.

Jeapes, Tony. *SAS Secret War: Operation Storm in the Middle East.* London: Greenhill Books, 2005.

Kitson, Frank. *Bunch of Five.* London: Faber and Faber Limited, 1977.

———. *Low Intensity Operations: Subversion, Insurgency, and Peacekeeping.* St. Petersburg, FL: Hailer Publishing, 2009.

Kolenda, Christopher. "AO Saber 1-91 CAV, 173d Airborne." U. S. Army Command Brief, August 1, 2008, 9.

McKeown, John. "Britain and Oman: The Dhofar War and Its Significance." PhD Dissertation, University of Cambridge, 1981.

Ray, Bryan. *Dangerous Frontiers: Campaigning in Somaliland and Oman.* South Yorkshire, England: Pen and Sword Books Ltd., 2008.

Sibley, Paul. *A Monk In The SAS: Second Edition.* London: Spiderwize Publishing, 2011.

Springer, Nathan. "Implementing a Population-centric Strategy in Northeast Afghanistan, May 07-July 08." *Small Wars Journal,* March 1, 2010. http://smallwarsjournal.com/blog/2010/03/implementing-a-populationcentr/. (accessed May 2, 2011)

Thompson, Robert. *Defeating Communist Insurgency.* St. Petersburg, FL: Hailer Publishing, 2005.

Trinquier, Roger. *Modern Warfare: A French View of Counterinsurgency.* Westport CT: Praeger Security International, 2006.

Tse-Tung, Mao. *On Guerrilla Warfare.* New York: Praegar Publishers, 1961.

Wilfurt, D.J. "Some Aspects of Anti-Terrorist Operations: Malaya." 22d Special Air Services Regiment, 7th Special Forces Group, Operational Assessment, 1963.

Documents, Letters, and Captured Enemy Material

Forster, J. M. "A Comparative Study of the Emergencies in Malaya and Kenya." *Operational Research Unit Far East* 1/57, 1957.

Headquarters Dhofar Salalah. "SAF Take-Over of Firqat – Dhofar." OPS/D/12 December 28, 1971, 2.

———. "Oman Operations: 1970-1975," 1975, 5.

McChrystal, Stanley. "Tactical Directive. Kabul, AF: International Security and Assistance Force, July 6, 2009.

———. "ISAF Commander's Counterinsurgency Guidance." Kabul, AF: International Security and Assistance Force, August 26, 2009.

——— . "ISAF Commander's Initial Assessment." Kabul, AF: International Security and Assistance Force, August 30, 2009.

——— ."ISAF Counterinsurgency Training Guidance." Kabul, AF: International Security and Assistance Force, November 10, 2009.

Middle East Center. "Origins and Formations of the Firqats." Oxford: St. Anthony's College, 1972, Annex A to Section 10, 2.

Doctrinal References

Army, Department of the. Field Manual 3-24, *Counterinsurgency.* Washington DC: Department of the Army, 2006.

——— . Field Manual 3-24.2, *Tactics in Counterinsurgency.* Washington DC: Department of the Army, 2009.

——— . Field Manual 31-16, *Counterguerrilla Operations.* Washington DC: Department of the Army, 1963.

Secondary Sources

Afsar, Shahid, and Chris Samples. "The Taliban: an organizational analysis." *Military Review* (May-June 2008): 58-73.

Andrade, Dale. "Westmoreland was right: learning the wrong lessons from the Vietnam War." *Small Wars and Insurgencies* 19, no. 2 (June 2008): 145-181.

Arnold, James. *Jungle of Snakes: A Century of Counterinsurgency Warfare from the Philippines to Iraq.* New York: Bloomsbury Press, 2009.

Barno, David. "Fighting the other war: counterinsurgency strategy in Afghanistan 2003-2005." *Military Review* (September-October 2007): 32-44.

Belasco, Amy. *RL33110, The Cost of Iraq, Afghanistan, and Other Global War On Terror Operations Since 9/11.* Washington, DC: Congressional Research Service, March 29, 2011.

Bergerud, Eric. *The Dynamics of Defeat: The Vietnam War in Hau Nghia Province.* Oxford: Westview Press, 1991.

Birtle, Andrew. *US Army Counterinsurgency and Contingency Operations Doctrine 1942-1976.* Washington, DC Center of Military History United States Army, 2007.

Bowman, Steven, and Catherine Dale. *War in Afghanistan: Strategy, Military Operations, and Issues for Congress.* Washington, DC: Congressional Research Service, June 8, 2010.

Bruno, Greg. "Winning the Information War in Afghanistan and Pakistan." *Council on Foreign Relations*, May 11, 2009. http://www.cfr.org/pakistan/winning-information-war-afghanistan-pakistan/p19330 (accessed April 30, 2011).

Burton, Brian, and John Nagl. "Learning as we go: the US Army adapts to COIN in Iraq, July 2004-December 2006." *Small Wars and Insurgencies* 19, no. 3 (September 2008): 303-327.

Caldwell, William and Steven Leonard. "Field Manual 3-07, Stability Operations: Upshifting the Engine of Change." *Military Review 88* (July/August 2008): 6.

Chiarelli, Peter, and Patrick Michaelis. "The Requirements for Full-Spectrum Operations." *Military Review*, 85, no. 4 (July-August 2005): 4-17.

Cilliers, J. K. *Counter-insurgency in Rhodesia.* London: Croom Helm Publishers, 1985.

Clausewitz, Carl Von. *On War.* Princeton, NJ: Princeton University Press, 1976.

Coates, John. *Suppressing Insurgency, An Analysis of the Malayan Emergency 1948-1954.* Boulder, CO: Westview Press, 1992.

Colvin, John. *Giap: Volcano Under Snow.* New York: Soho Press, Inc., 1996.

Comber, Leon. *Malaya's Secret Police 1945-60: The Role of Special Branch in the Malayan Emergency.* Pasir Panjang, Singapore: Institute of Southeast Asian Studies, 2008.

Creveld, Martin Van. *The Art of War: War and Military Thought.* Washington, DC: Smithsonian Books, 2005.

Deane-Drummond, A.J. "Brilliant but little known British Desert Action: Operations in Oman." *The Times,* April 9, 1959.

Dixon, Paul. "Hearts and minds? British counterinsurgency strategy in Northern Ireland." *Journal of Strategic Studies* 32, no. 3 (June 2009): 445-474.

Dorronsoro, Gilles. *Revolution Unending: Afghanistan 1979 to the Present.* New York: Columbia University Press, 2005.

Edwards, David. *Heroes of the Age: Moral Fault Lines on the Afghan Frontier.* Los Angeles: University of California Press, 1996.

Gentile, Gian. "A Strategy of Tactics: Population-centric COIN and the Army." *Parameters* (Autumn 2009): 5-17.

Grau, Lester, and Ali Ahmad Jalali. *The Other Side of the Mountain: Mujahideen Tactics in the Soviet-Afghan War.* Quantico, Virginia: USMC Studies and Analysis Division, 1995.

Green, T. N. *The Guerrilla—Selections from the Marine Corps Gazette.* New York: Praeger Publishing, 1962, 37-54 and 147-177.

Hack, Karl. "The Malayan Emergency as Counter-Insurgency Paradigm." *Journal of Strategic* Studies 32, no. 3 (2009):385.

Hammes, Thomas. *The Sling and the Stone: On War in the 21st Century.* St Paul, MN: MBI Publishing Company, 2006.

Haroon, Sana. *Frontier of Faith: Islam in the Indo-Afghan Borderland.* New York: Columbia University Press, 2007.

Hart, Peter. *The I.R.A. at War 1916-1923.* Oxford: Oxford University Press, 2003.

Haycock, Ronald, *Regular Armies and Insurgency.* London: Croom Helm Publishing, 1979.

Heggoy, Alf. *Insurgency and Counterinsurgency in Algeria.* Bloomington, IN: Indiana University Press, 1972.

Hewitt, Steve. *The British War on Terror.* New York: Continuum Publishing, 2008.

Hoffman, Bruce. *"Lessons for Contemporary Counterinsurgencies: The Rhodesian Experience."* Santa Monica, CA: The RAND Corporation, 1992.

Hoffman, Bruce. *Lessons for Contemporary Counterinsurgencies: The Rhodesian Experience.* Santa Monica, CA: The RAND Corporation, 1992.

Hoffman, Frank. "Neo-Classical Counter-insurgency?" *Parameters* (Summer 2007): 71-87.

Hopkinson, Michael. *The Irish War of Independence.* Montreal: McGill-Queen's University Press, 2002.

Hunt, Richard. *Pacification: The American Struggle for Vietnam's Hearts and Minds.* Boulder, CO: Westview Press, 1995.

International Security and Assistance Force Command. "Mission Statement." Website. http://www.isaf.nato.int/mission.html (accessed May 2, 2011).

Johnson, Thomas, and Chris Mason. "No Sign until the Burst of Fire: Understanding the Pakistan-Afghanistan Frontier", *International Security* 32, no. 4 (Spring 2008): 41-77.

Jomini, Baron De. *The Art of War.* El Paso, TX: Norte Press, 2005.

Katzman, Kenneth. *RL30588, Afghanistan: Post-Taliban Governance, Security, and US Policy. Washington, DC: Congressional Research Service, 11.*

Kilcullen, David. *The Accidental Guerrilla.* Oxford: Oxford University Press, 2009.

———. *Counterinsurgency.* United Kingdom: Oxford University Press, 2010.

Kolenda, Christopher. "Winning Afghanistan at the Community Level." *Joint Forces Quarterly* 56 (2010): 25-31.

Komer, R.W. *"The Malayan Emergency in Retrospect: Organization of a Successful Counterinsurgency Effort." Research Project, RAND, 1972.*

Komer, Robert. *Bureaucracy at War: US Performance in the Vietnam Conflict.* Boulder, CO: Westview Press, 1986.

Krepinevich, Andrew. *The Army and Vietnam.* Baltimore, MD: Johns Hopkins University Press, 1986.

Kriger, Norma. *Zimbabwe's Guerrilla War.* Cambridge: Cambridge University Press, 1993.

Linn, Brian. *The Philippine War, 1899-1902.* Lawrence, KS: University of Kansas Press, 2000.

Ludwig, Walter. "Supporting allies in counterinsurgency: Britain and the Dhofar Rebellion." *Small Wars and Insurgencies* 19, no. 1 (2008): 53-81.

Lustick, Ian. *Trapped in the War on Terror.* Philadelphia, PA: University of Pennsylvania Press, 2006.

MacKinlay, John. *"Rethinking Counterinsurgency." RAND Counterinsurgency Study 5, 2008, 43-63.*

Mackinlay, John. *The Insurgent Archipelago.* London: Hurst and Company Publishers, 2009.

Malevich, John, and Daryl Youngman. "The Afghan Balance of Power and the Culture of Jihad." *Military Review* (May-June 2011): 35.

Malkasian, Carter. "The Role of Perceptions and Political reform in Counterinsurgency: The Case of Western Iraq, 2004-2005." *Small Wars and Insurgencies* 17, no. 3 (September 2006): 367-394.

Margesson, Rhoda. United Nations Assistance Mission in Afghanistan: Background and Policy Issues. Washington, DC: Congressional Research Service, December 27, 2010.

Markel, Wade. "Draining the Swamp: The British Strategy of Population Control." *Parameters*, Spring 2006, 35-48. http://www.carlisle.army.mil/ usawc/ Parameters/06spring/markel.htm. (Accessed May 12, 2011).

Marston, Daniel, and Carter Malkasian. *Counterinsurgency in Modern Warfare*. Oxford: Osprey Publishing, 2010.

Marston, Daniel. "Adaptation in the Field: The British Army's Difficult Campaign in Iraq." *Security Challenges*, Vol. 6, no. 1 (Autumn 2010): 71-84.

————. "Lost and found in the jungle." In *Big Wars and Small Wars*, ed. Hew Strachan. London: Routledge Publishing, 2006.

McCoy, Alfred. *Policing America's Empire*. Madison, WI: University of Wisconsin Press, 2009.

McCuen, John. *The Art of Counter-Revolutionary Warfare*. Harrisburg, PA: Stackpole Books, 1972.

Metz, Steve. "New Challenges and Old Concepts: Understanding 21st Century Insurgency." *Parameters* (Winter 2007-08):20-32.

Meyerle, Jerry, Megan Katt, and Jim Gavrilis, CRM D0022894.A2. "Counterinsurgency on the Ground in Afghanistan: How different units adapted to local conditions." Center of Navy Analysis, July 1, 2010, 51-64.

Miers, Richard. *Shoot to Kill*. London: Faber and Faber Publishing, 1959.

Millen, Raymond. "Time for a Strategic and Intellectual Pause in Afghanistan." *Parameters* (Summer 2010): 6-19.

Moyano, Maria. *Argentina's Lost Patrol: Armed Struggle 1969-1979*. New Haven, CT: Yale University Press, 1995.

Nagl, John. A Better War in Afghanistan: Senate Committee on Foreign Relations. Alexandria, VA: Center for New American Security, September 16, 2009.

Naylor, Sean, and Michael Hoffman, "Petraeus Reviews, clarifies strike directive." Air Force Times, August 9, 2010. http://www.airforcetimes.

com/news/2010/08/ airforce_rules_of_engagement_080910/. (Accessed 18 May 2011).

O'Neill, Mark. Confronting the Hydra. Sydney, Australia: Lowy Institute Study, 2009.

O'Neill, Robert. *General Giap: Politician and Strategist.* New York: Praegar Publishers, 1969.

Omrani, Bijan. "The Durand Line: History and Problems of the Afghan-Pakistan Border." *Asian Affairs* 40, no. 2 (July 2009): 177-195

Paget, Julian. *Counter-Insurgency Operations.* New York: Walker and Company, 1967.

Paret, Peter. *French Revolutionary Warfare from Indochina to Algeria: The Analysis of a Political and Military Doctrine.* London: Pall Mall Press, 1964.

Paret, Peter. *Makers of Modern Strategy.* Princeton, NJ: Princeton University Press, 1986.

Pye, Lucian. *Lessons From The Malayan Struggle Against Communism.* Cambridge, MA: Center for International Studies, Massachusetts Institute of Technology, 1957.

Race, Jeffrey. *War Comes to Long An.* California: UC Press, 1972.

Ramsey, Robert. *Savage Wars of Peace: Case Studies of Pacification in the Philippines, 1900-1902.* Fort Leavenworth, KS: Combat Studies Institute, 2007.

Roy, Oliver. *Islam and Resistance in Afghanistan: Second Edition.* Cambridge, England: Cambridge University Press, 1990.

Rozen, Laura. "Winning hearts and minds: all of McChrystal's advisors." *Foreign Policy,* July 31, 2009. http://thecable.foreignpolicy.com/posts/2009/07/31/ winning_hearts_and_minds_all_of_mcchrystals_advisors. (accessed May 8, 2011).

Rubin, Barnett, and Ahmed Rashid. "The Great Game to the Great Bargain." *Foreign Affairs* 87, no. 6 (November/December 2008): 30-44.

Sandu, K.S. "Emergency Resettlement in Malaya." *Journal of Tropical Geography* 18 (1964): 157-183.

Selth, Andrew. "Ireland and insurgency: the lessons of history." *Small Wars & Insurgency* 2, no. 2 (1991): 299-322.

Strachan, Hew. *Big Wars and Small Wars.* London: Routledge, 2006.

Thornton, Rod. "Getting it wrong: the crucial mistakes made in the early stages of the British Army's deployment to Northern Ireland." *Journal of Strategic Studies* 30, no. 1 (February 2007):73-107.

Townshend, Charles. "The IRA and the Development of Guerrilla Warfare, 1916-1921," *English Historical Review* 94 (April 1979): 318-345.

Tripodi, Christian. "Good for one but not the other; The Sandeman System of Pacification as Applied to Baluchistan and the North-West Frontier, 1877-1947." *The Journal of Military History* 73, no. 3 (July 2009): 767-802.

Tzu, Sun. *The Art of War.* London: Oxford University Press, 1963.

Ucko, David. *The New Counterinsurgency Era: Transforming the US Military for Modern Wars.* Washington DC: Georgetown University Press, 2009.

Wade Markel. "Draining the Swamp: The British Strategy of Population Control." *Parameters*, (Spring 2006): 37-62.

White House. "Remarks by the President in Address to the Nation on the Way Forward in Afghanistan and Pakistan." Office of the Press Secretary, December 1, 2009.

Willbanks, James. *Abandoning Vietnam.* Lawrence, KS: University of Kansas Press, 2004.